WITTGENSTEIN

A BEGINNER'S GUIDE

WITTGENSTEIN

A BEGINNER'S GUIDE

Hodder & Stoughton

A MEMBER OF THE HODDER HEADLINE GROUP

Orders: please contact Bookpoint Ltd, 130 Milton Park, Abingdon, Oxon OX14 4SB. Telephone: (44) 01235 400400, Fax: (44) 01235 400500. Lines are open from 9.00–6.00, Monday to Saturday, with a 24-hour message answering service. Email address: orders@bookpoint.co.uk

British Library Cataloguing in Publication Data
A catalogue record for this title is available from The British Library

ISBN 0 340 80399 1

First published 2001
Impression number   10 9 8 7 6 5 4 3 2 1
Year 2007 2006 2005 2004 2003 2002 2001

Cover photo from AKG
Cover illustration by Jacey
Typeset by Transet Limited, Coventry, England.
Printed in Great Britain for Hodder & Stoughton Educational, a division of Hodder Headline Plc, 338 Euston Road, London NW1 3BH by Cox & Wyman, Reading, Berks.

CONTENTS

'Show me what you are searching for and I will tell you what you are looking for.'

Wittgenstein, *Philosophical Investigations*

Introduction

This book is a guide to the life and times of the philosopher Wittgenstein, the course of development that characterized his philosophical thinking, and the influence of his work on contemporary thought.

Wittgenstein was a remarkable person in many different ways. He was born in Austria and as a solider in World War I his army rucksack was stuffed with a copy of what was soon to be published as the *Tractatus*, a seminal work of philosophy that created ripples of excitement amongst a number of European intellectuals. At Cambridge, Wittgenstein developed over time a new philosophy that was spread more by word of mouth than any published work and it was only after his death in 1951 that his *Philosophical Publications* was published.

Both the *Tractatus* and *Philosophical Investigations* are important and interesting works but they are not the kind of books that one can easily just pick up and start reading. This guide provides the necessary background information that will enable readers to grasp some of the essential concepts that will make the *Tractatus and Philosophical Investigations* less daunting books to encounter. Wittgenstein's biography is as fascinating as his philosophy and this guide also offers an account of his singular journey through life.

Who was Wittgenstein?

WHY IS WITTGENSTEIN IMPORTANT?

Wittgenstein is important because of the original way he explored a number of philosophical issues. In his early philosophy, his central question was this: How is language possible? This is not a question about the physiological process of making noises using the tongue but a philosophical inquiry about how language can be used to say something about the world. Another way of putting this question would be: What is the relationship between language and the world? Philosophers before Wittgenstein had concerned themselves with the nature of language, but when they did so it was as part of larger questions and concerns thst interested them. Wittgenstein, on the other hand, remained focused on an extraordinary aspect of life that hadn't struck others as extraordinary. Here we are in a world where so much exists, including other people, and where things change and move, appear and disappear and so on, and included in all this are some particular bits of the world, what we call language, being used to represent other bits of the world. From this phenomenon of language so much that we understand, so much that makes us human beings, comes about. How does it do this and what is going on in the process? What is thought, for is it possible to think without language? If we think about questions like the meaning of life, if we ask ourselves why is there something rather than nothing, what answers can language provide?

In an striking manner, as we shall see, the life Wittgenstein chose to live is inseparable from the philosophical questions he confronted. Certain questions possessed him, drove him to contemplate suicide when he was young, urged him to behaviour that is as fascinating as it is odd, and led him to express his ideas in two remarkable books: the *Tractatus*, published in 1921, and *Philosophical Investigations*, published posthumously in 1953.

The *Tractatus* is a work of literature that speaks to us in a highly individual way. It does not use continuous prose but reads like the sonorous messages that came from the oracular shrines of ancient Greece: cryptic, pregnant, aphoristic. Its remarkable style makes the text a modernist work of art, obsessed with its own medium – language in this case – and declaring the autonomy of language. The *Tractatus* strives to express thoughts – about the nature of language and reality and the mystery at the heart of existence – that the book itself proclaims are unsayable. Despite these momentous claims, and the initial difficulty of getting to grips with the style of the *Tractatus*, it is not a book that could be described as pretentious or boastful.

If Wittgenstein's early text is modernist in spirit and execution, then *Philosophical Investigations* is a **postmodern** work of art. The book resembles a series of fragments, pieces of conversation, with no chapter titles or contents page or helpful summaries. The author is no longer seduced by the idea that a binding pattern locks reality and language into a matrix. There is no fond belief in a crystalline order, a logical essence, at the heart of our language world. The meaning of a word, instead, is to be found in the way it is used, the meaning is to be found in the **language-game** to which the word belongs. Philosophical problems arise when this is forgotten or when one language-game is confused with another

KEYWORDS

Postmodern: a self-awareness in art of the forms of art themselves; the tendency in literature, architecture and other arts to adopt an ironic attitude towards their own identity.

Language-game: a term introduced by Wittgenstein to highlight the way in which language use is a form of social, rule-governed activity bounded by a context and a set of human purposes.

one that functions in a different way. Similarities in the form of particular uses of language create problems. For example, it makes obvious sense to ask 'Where is my suitcase?' but it makes no sense to ask 'Where is my toothache?' We can understand a question like 'What is a washing machine?' but we can't understand a question like 'What is beauty?' in the same sort of way. To think of these last two questions in the same sort of way is to be betrayed by a surface similarity in grammar.

Wittgenstein's importance arises from his preoccupation with the nature of language and one would have to go back to ancient Greece to find other philosophers who explored language and the meaning of words with such rigour and insight. It is to Wittgenstein we owe what has been called the 'linguistic turn', the twentieth-century's recognition that questions concerning language are inseparable from the traditional philosophical pursuit of questions about truth and knowledge. In 1998 a poll of professional philosophers elected Wittgenstein as the world's fifth most important thinker in their field, eclipsed only by Aristotle, Plato, Kant and Nietzsche. This gives some idea of the enormous influence exerted by a philosopher who published only one slim text in his own lifetime.

A BRIEF BIOGRAPHY

Ludwig Wittgenstein was born in late imperial Vienna in 1889 into a super-rich family, one of the wealthiest in the whole of Austria; the family home in central Vienna had a total of six grand pianos for invited musicians to choose from when they attended a soirée. Wittgenstein became interested in philosophy while studying mechanical engineering in Manchester and he went to Cambridge to study under the renowned Bertrand Russell. When World War I broke out in 1914, Wittgenstein volunteered for service in the Austrian army and it was while serving as a soldier that his *Tractatus Logico-Philosophicus*, usually just called the *Tractatus*, was completed.

Wittgenstein became depressed by the sense that, as far as he could tell, no one understood a book that he thought had said everything about philosophy that could be meaningfully expressed in words. There followed ten years of withdrawal from philosophical life when he worked, amongst other things, as a village school-teacher, an amateur architect and a gardener in a monastery. During this time, his *Tractatus* was taken up by a group of philosophers known as the Vienna Circle and had a tremendous influence on their thinking. Towards the end of the 1920s, Wittgenstein returned to academic life in Cambridge and to the study of philosophy, fuelled now by a growing realization that the *Tractatus* was not the final word on philosophy.

During the 1930s, Wittgenstein developed a new philosophy and just before the outbreak of World War II in 1939 he was appointed Professor of Philosophy at Cambridge. He insisted on contributing to the war effort and worked as a porter and then a technician in hospitals before returning with reluctance to Cambridge to resume his professorship. Within a couple of years, though, he resigned from the post and went to live in Ireland where he stayed for 18 months. Bothered by ill health, he was finally diagnosed with cancer and died in 1951 in the home of his doctor where he had been cared for by the doctor's wife. The last remark of his last text, *On Certainty*, was written the day before he lapsed into unconsciousness and died.

WHAT WAS HE LIKE?

Wittgenstein possessed a tremendous intellectual charisma that left a deep impression on most people who got to know him. He was of medium height, with penetrating blue eyes, and he inspired adoration from many impressionable students, some of whom imitated his characteristic manner of dress: open-necked shirt, never a tie, tweedy jacket, flannel trousers. A nervous, intense energy fuelled his style of lecturing, revealed in anxiety lines across the forehead and anguished silences, broken by questions or reproaches like 'God I am stupid today'. He loathed academic life and was often scornful of intellectuals, especially if they were philosophers. 'Don't try to shit higher than your arse', was Wittgenstein's contemptuous comment on philosophers who aspired to insights they were incapable of holding. What has been said so far might give the impression that Wittgenstein was a theatrical kind of individual but this would be very misleading. He was an extremely private person, often uneasy with the opposite sex, taking no part in public life, publishing remarkably little and shunning exposure. For a long time his work was known only within a narrow circle of professional philosophers and it is only within the last few decades that his thought has made a broader impact. For over 20 years, between his return to academic life in 1929 and the publication of *Philosophical Investigations* in 1953, the influence of his later philosophy was known only through his students at Cambridge.

Wittgenstein was an intensely moral person. In the 1930s he returned to the village in Austria where he had taught in order to seek out pupils he had physically punished in the classroom and apologize to them personally. This was not done in a spirit of arrogant pride; the experience was a painful one for him to see through but he did it because he felt it was the right way to behave. Ethics for Wittgenstein was not a topic for dry academic discourse, it was an obligation to make the right choices for a good and honest life.

Some of those who could claim to know Wittgenstein have left accounts of their perceptions of him that confirm this impression of his highly moral nature. The literary critic F. R. Leavis recalled how one day, meeting his philosopher friend in Cambridge, he was summarily informed by him that he must give up literary criticism. This was not out of character for Wittgenstein, and there are cases where he actively dissuaded his own students at Cambridge from pursuing philosophy as a profession. He wanted those he cared about to do a decent job in life, practising medicine or becoming a manual labourer, and not waste their time as academics in a university. For Wittgenstein, manual labour was a supreme example of the good life and he idealized it as the model of virtuous living. This partly explains his interest in Soviet Russia, a country he visited in 1935 with the intention of returning to live there as a doctor. Wittgenstein admired Russia's ability to provide employment for everyone and approved of its principled commitment to removing class differences. Wittgenstein was not a politically minded person and his interest in Russian Communism was more ethical than ideological.

Wittgenstein's deep antagonism to academia led to him periodically abandoning his teaching post at Cambridge and trying out alternative professions or removing himself to isolated corners of Ireland and Norway. He said there was no oxygen in Cambridge. There is something remarkably likeable about this strange man. For all his intensity and fervour he also shows a disarming ordinariness that sets him far apart from the general type of highly talented person who becomes driven by a set of beliefs, philosophical or otherwise. Every now and again, the stereotype of the abstracted and intellectual philosopher is shattered by the realization that here is someone we can recognize as human and vulnerable. His loathing of academic life and armchair philosophy (taken literally, preferring deckchairs in his teaching room at Cambridge) was heartfelt and he was happier reading a thriller or watching a Western or a musical than socializing with fellow lecturers. He usually preferred the company of ordinary working people to that of cloistered intellectuals.

As Wittgenstein lay dying in 1951, his last words are reported to have been, 'Tell them I've had a wonderful life'. This message for his friends, who were on their way to see him, is often at odds with the impression of Wittgenstein as an intensely repressed and anguished individual. He is often viewed as a man tortured by his homosexuality, although there seems to be only one known case of a physical relationship with a lover. What is not in doubt is that sexuality bothered him and the relationship between sex and love vexed him throughout his life. His asceticism is one more aspect of his intensely moral nature, born of his deep loneliness and his tragic awareness of loss. The early death of a close friend in 1918 continued to haunt him and a second premature death of a friend in 1941 drove him to distraction. At one stage he thought of marrying a woman in Austria but it was conceived, by him at least, as a purely platonic marriage.

Wittgenstein was a complex character: intolerant, monkish, mystic, demanding, a perfectionist whose fastidiousness verged on the obsessive. He could be disconcertingly abrupt and, surprisingly for

abandoned this attitude and, although not so directly addressed in his later philosophy, there is no mistaking its continuing presence in his thought.

Wittgenstein's objection to traditional philosophy can be expressed in terms of his antipathy to its claims to explain matters, its endeavour to get to the essential foundations of philosophical matters. This, he came to realize, was the mistake of his early philosophy as expressed in the *Tractatus*. It wasn't that he felt that everything he said in that work was wrong; the flaw as he saw it was that he built up a general theory on the basis of what were particular insights. He never abandoned entirely the usefulness of regarding a sentence as a picture, but he did abandon the notion that *all* sentences, language itself, could be understood in this way. He abandoned the need to generalize, to look for some all-embracing essence that lay beneath the surface. Philosophy, he comes to see, is not about foundations, and questions like 'What is knowledge?' do not have the kind of foundational significance that traditional philosophy accords them. He points out that people go about their lives quite meaningfully, consulting their watches and filling appointment diaries, without needing to answer a question like 'What is time?'. We can know all sorts of things without knowing what knowing is, just as we can spell lots of words without having to be able to spell 'spelling'. From the absence of this need to provide foundations, new insights arose and it is the exploration of these new insights that constitutes his later philosophy.

✱ ✱ ✱*SUMMARY*✱ ✱ ✱

• Wittgenstein is important because of questions he asked about language and its relation to the world. His responses come in highly individual works of literature. The *Tractatus* expresses his early philosophy and *Philosophical Investigation* his later philosophy.

• In the *Tractatus*, language is seen as able to logically mirror the way things are in the world.

• *Philosophical Investigations* explores how language operates within a public, social community, a community that has rules for the use of words.

A Strange Young Life

2

A FREUDIAN CHILDHOOD

Ludwig Wittgenstein was born in Vienna in April 1889 into a fabulously rich family. Vienna's most famous doctor, Sigmund Freud, was working in the city and developing his theory of the unconscious in a society where he was able to study the sexual currents that churned disturbingly beneath the surface calm of bourgeois propriety. Wittgenstein's family mirrored the contradictory tensions of the **fin de siècle** Vienna that so fascinated Freud. On the surface, the family was the paragon of bourgeois contentment. Ludwig's father was a self-made millionaire, a plutocrat who had built up a vastly lucrative steel industry, while his mother's talent lay in music. The result was an extremely wealthy and cultured family where a musical evening with Brahms or Mahler as a guest was not unusual and where the artist Klimt could oblige Wittgenstein's sister with a wedding portrait for her marriage.

The Wittgenstein family may have been prodigiously successful in the eyes of society, but within it the **Freudian** worm of repression was hard at work. The oldest son, Hans, inherited his mother's extraordinary musical talent only to find his artistic vocation denied by his business-minded father. Fleeing to America, Hans died when Ludwig was only 13, having apparently thrown himself off a boat in Chesapeake Bay. By this time another brother, Rudolf, had left home for Berlin where later, tortured by angst over his homosexuality it seems, he played out a macabre public suicide. Buying a drink for a café pianist, he requested his favourite song, 'I am Lost', and listened to it as he sat dying from the cyanide he had swallowed. A third brother would also die by his own hand during World War I.

A broader form of denial characterized the family's attitude towards its Jewishness, with Ludwig's paternal grandparents converting from Judaism to Protestantism. Indeed, Ludwig's father, by marrying a half-Jewish woman, had to disobey his own father's injunction to his children not to wed Jews. An intriguing aspect of the family's history arose from the decision to send the young Ludwig, who was thought to share's his father's talent and interest in engineering, not to the grammar school in Vienna but to a less academic and more technical-oriented school in Linz. The young Wittgenstein, who after 14 years of private education at home was hardly at ease with his working-class peers, stayed there for only three years, but for one of those years, 1904–5, he shared the playground with another student at the same institution, a young boy called Adolf Hitler.

THE JEW OF LINZ MEETS RUSSELL

The evidence is purely circumstantial, but there are grounds for thinking that the young Wittgenstein could have been the boy that Hitler refers to in *Mein Kampf*. Hitler writes that his first personal encounter with a Jew involved an odd boy at his school in Linz, and the possibility that this boy was Wittgenstein has been argued for in a book entitled *The Jew of Linz*. The author's further claim, that the philosopher went on to become Moscow's top level recruiting agent at Cambridge for Communist spies, may be treated more circumspectly but back in the Linz playground the privileged life of the Wittgenstein boy certainly isolated him within the school and Hitler may well have known and been affected by him.

From Linz, Wittgenstein went on to study engineering in Berlin; to all intents and purposes destined to follow in his father's footsteps and become a captain of industry. From Berlin, in 1908, Wittgenstein went to Manchester University to study aeronautical engineering and, in the course of studying the mathematics, found himself introduced to Bertrand Russell's *The Principles of Mathematics*. This book changed the course of his life because the young engineer became totally absorbed by Russell's intention to show that mathematics can be derived from logical principles.

Eventually, in 1911, Wittgenstein made a visit to **Frege**, a German mathematician who was also working on the relationship between mathematics and logic. Frege's recommendation, that the young engineer should go to Cambridge and study under Russell, was taken very literally and in October of that year the young Wittgenstein knocked on the door of Russell's rooms in Trinity College. The young Austrian wanted confirmation that he could do philosophy. By January, when Russell had a chance to read Wittgenstein's ideas in writing, the Cambridge lecturer was impressed – 'Perhaps he will do great things'- and it was with relief that Wittgenstein, aged 22, abandoned engineering and embraced philosophy. It was also the beginning of a long and tumultuous relationship between Russell and Wittgenstein, on the personal as well as the professional level. Their relationship began with Russell as the academic supervisor but he was soon to feel eclipsed by his brilliant student, 'Perhaps the most perfect example I have ever known of genius as traditionally conceived, passionate, profound, intense, and dominating'.

KEYWORDS

Frege: Gottlob Frege (1848–1925), German mathematician, logician and philosopher. He was little appreciated in his own lifetime, but is now regarded as the founder of modern mathematical logic and the philosophy of language.

Keynes: John Maynard Keynes (1883–1946), English economist, proponent of state-managed full employment under a capitalist system.

FROM CAMBRIDGE TO NORWAY

Wittgenstein's first spell at Cambridge was brief but charged with significance. He formed a deep friendship with a mathematics undergraduate, David Pinsent, and came to know John Maynard **Keynes**. His undergraduate friend would be killed in an accident during World War I while Keynes was to remain a life-long friend. On the philosophical front, the single-minded Wittgenstein advanced at a lightening pace and by 1913 Russell had conceded authority to him in the field of logic. When this happened, Wittgenstein was only 24 and officially just an undergraduate of the university.

While on holiday in Norway, Wittgenstein was seized with the idea of escaping from the bourgeois society of Cambridge where socially he did not feel at ease. He wanted to be alone, in a remote land like Norway, where he could think unhindered. Never one to dally when an idea took hold, Wittgenstein bade farewell to academia and by the end of 1913 was secluded in a Norwegian village by the side of a fjord. He philosophized intently, alone, feeling driven to excavate the nature of logic until its foundations were revealed. Only then, he felt, would he find the philosophic key that would unlock all the problems of logic and put his own head to rest. Describing his mind as 'on fire', Wittgenstein battled with his thoughts and paused only when the summer season arrived and he felt he had to flee from the tourists. He returned to Vienna only to find that the outbreak of World War I had scuppered his plan to go back in the autumn to Norway and write.

FACING DEATH

Wittgenstein volunteered as an ordinary soldier for Austria in World War I but his motive was not simply one of patriotism. Although Wittgenstein was never an orthodox Christian, at this stage he was in a highly

KEYWORD

A priori: what is known independent of experience.

religious state of mind and welcomed the prospect of confronting death in battle. He felt it would be spiritually testing and a potentially liberating experience. His immediate feelings when thrown into the company of other soldiers were very different. He felt as if he was back in school in Linz, vulnerable because of his difference and disgusted at the coarseness of humanity. His diary entries show him grappling with philosophy – asking himself whether an **a priori** order exists in the world and if so in what does it consist – unable to discuss the issues with his English friends for his country was now at war with England.

Wittgenstein was still concerned with the nature of logic but, left to himself and the experience of war, an element of **mysticism** was making itself felt. The book that would emerge, the *Tractatus*, would be a unique synthesis of logic and mysticism.

KEYWORD

Mysticism: a meaning that is hidden, mysterious, spiritually apprehensible.

Being at the war front, something he had requested and longed for, meant that Wittgenstein faced the very real possibility of death. He even asked for the most dangerous posting, manning an observation post facing the enemy, desiring to test himself by going to the edge. In such extreme circumstances, Wittgenstein completed his thoughts about logic, language and reality. Extreme too was his conclusion that the mystery and mysticism at the heart of existence place an absolute limit on what can be said in philosophy.

'Yes, my work has broadened out from the foundations of logic to the essence of the world'

FROM RICHES TO RAGS

After the death of his father in 1913, Wittgenstein became a very rich individual; just how rich he was may be judged by the fact that descendants of the family are still living off the fortune. Wittgenstein was probably the single richest person amongst the 300,000 Austrians taken prisoner at the end of the war. He rebuffed the attempts of his family to pull strings to get him released early and waited with his fellow soldiers until August 1919 to be liberated. Once back in Vienna, he set about disentangling himself from the burden, as he saw it, of inherited wealth. He ordered the transfer of all his wealth to his three sisters and a brother and insisted that no loophole should remain that could possibly leave him with a claim on any part of the money. It was, as one of the officials handling the paperwork pointed out, an act of financial suicide. No matter, to Wittgenstein it was a necessary act because he had to live his life according to his own deeply felt principles. Not that he was happy and content. David Pinsent, his best friend, was dead while he, a 30-year-old ex-soldier and author of a philosophical treatise that he felt no one would understand, only felt sure of the fact that he never wanted to return to academic life.

✷ ✷ ✷ SUMMARY ✷ ✷ ✷

● Wittgenstein had a privileged upbringing in a highly cultured and wealthy Viennese family. In his adolescence, two of his older brothers committed suicide. At the age of 14 he was sent to a technical school in Linz.

● At secondary school he was a contemporary of Hitler. Although there is no record of them having known each other, Wittgenstein may be the Jew that Hitler refers to in *Mein Kampf*.

● Studying aeronautical engineering in England, he developed an interest in the foundations of mathematics and went to Cambridge to ask Russell if he was any good at philosophy. Recognizing his talent, Russell encouraged him and Wittgenstein stayed at Cambridge until 1913 when he left to think alone in Norway.

● Volunteering to fight at the front in World War I, Wittgenstein experienced the proximity of death; a mystical element finds its way into his study of the nature of logic and the world.

● At the end of the war his book, the *Tractatus*, is published. The entire vast fortune he had inherited on the death of his father is given away.

Throwing Away the Ladder 3

THE LURE OF LOGIC

Logic is the science of reasoning and a logical argument is one that builds on what has gone before in such a way as to seem incapable of being refuted. The idea that there is something compelling about the nature and application of logic is suggested in expressions like 'the logic of events' or 'logic dictates that…'. The mathematician and philosopher Frege recognized logic as something unique and saw it as the basis of arithmetic. He went further than this and allied logic with the nature of truth itself, writing that logical laws are indeed the laws of truth. Such laws he viewed as being like boundary stones which cannot be displaced, absolute truths remaining true whatever the stray happenings of the material world. Frege wrote, 'If it is true that I am writing this in my study on the 13th of July 1893 while the wind howls outside, then it is true even should all men later hold it to be false'. Logic is truth and it is unaffected by what people think or sense. In the idiom of philosophy, the sense of this last sentence is expressed by saying logic is independent of a knowing subject. The anarchist physicist Shevek, in Ursula La Guin's novel *The Dispossessed*, expresses a similar idea when he says to himself, 'If a book were written all in numbers, it would be true'.

Wittgenstein, only 22 when he visited Frege, was becoming fascinated by the notion that logic opened a door to eternal truths that remained independent of a knowing subject. He was fired by the possibility that to study

> **KEYWORD**
>
> Metaphysics: the study of the ultimate nature of reality.

logic was to study the form of reality itself: 'In logic there are no surprises' he would come to say. He was to pursue his study relentlessly, driven by the need for a satisfying **metaphysics**, but the conclusions he came to while contemplating his own death in war would go well beyond what Frege and Russell were saying.

STYLE OF THE *TRACTATUS*

The full title of Wittgenstein's book, which first appeared in German in 1921 and in an English translation the following year, is *Tractatus Logico-Philosophicus*. It is not a massive tome, the standard English translation by Pears and McGuinness is only 70 pages, but the extremely compressed style of writing makes demands on the reader quite out of proportion to its length.

The book is a series of statements, numbered in decimal notation, amounting to only seven propositions bearing whole numbers. However, like a Russian doll, there are layers within layers and the sub-divisions build up an elaborate structure. The numbered statements that make up the text read like aphorisms, with metaphors and similes appearing at crucial moments. The resulting style of writing is remarkably concise and we will look at the first few pages to see this oracular style at work. This will give some idea of Wittgenstein's style and at the same time unpack some of the book's early statements that provide a foundation for what is to follow.

The first proposition bearing a whole number tells us that 'The world is all that is the case'. This is the proposition in its entirety. There is nothing else by way of elucidation, and although the sense is baffling the language is plain and direct. The first sub-division, numbered 1.1 in the text, says that the world is the 'totality of facts'. The second proposition bearing a whole number tells that 'What is the case – a fact – is the existence of states of affairs'. Without being sure of exactly what is meant here, there is a comfortable air of realism about it. The world is made up of facts and although we can't be certain what is meant by states of affairs this term has a reassuring, down-to-earth feel. There is a world out there, says Wittgenstein, and it's real.

The next statement, numbered 2.01, asserts that a state of affairs is 'a combination of objects' and almost a dozen propositions then follow that elaborate on this statement. We are told that objects not only have the possibility of combining with other objects but that this possibility of forming combinations is built into the nature of objects. This, we shall see, is regarded by Wittgenstein as a fundamental aspect of the logical nature of the world. Objects have a potential for occurring in states of affairs and this potential for forming combinations is defined as the 'form' of an object. Reality, then, is not made up of discreet bits and pieces but of objects forming structures. These structures arise through the combinations that objects have the possibility of making.

Further propositions follow about the nature of objects and how they combine. This leads to the statement numbered 2.03, where a simile is used to stress the logical nature of the ways in which objects can combine: 'In a state of affairs objects fit into one another like the links of a chain'.

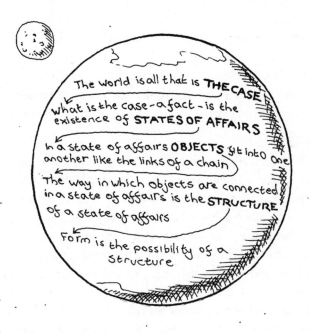

The illustration uses Wittgenstein's words from the *Tractatus* to summarize the first four pages of his book. The importance of its description of the world will soon emerge when we see that Wittgenstein sees language as being able to represent the world as it has been described here. These opening pages of the *Tractatus* are also typical of Wittgenstein's style in a number of ways. Wittgenstein does not produce any arguments to show how one point leads to another. Propositions are stated, images are employed, and a lot is left unexplained. What exactly are the objects that make up reality? They are simple and unalterable so they are not things like hammers or geraniums but are they raw sense data, or the elementary particles of physics? And is the determination of their form, their possibilities for forming structures, a reference to the laws of physics? The answers to these questions are contested by professional philosophers. What remains undisputed is the sense of compulsion with which Wittgenstein asserts that there is an a priori order to the world. It is not a chaotic mess, objects exist in relationships and they have a definite scope. Later in his life, Wittgenstein will question his belief in the nature of logic but for now his conviction is that there is an order to the world that is independent of experience.

PICTURING REALITY

From a Paris traffic-court, where a traffic accident was modelled using toys and dolls to represent how the incident occurred, Wittgenstein apparently got the idea that is next developed in the *Tractatus*. It occupies statements numbered 2.1 to 2.225, bringing the second main proposition of the book to an end, and introduces the idea of a picture. The elements of a picture, we are told, are the representatives of objects. For example, the lines and shading that make up a drawing of a cat in a picture represent the feline creature we call a cat. Secondly, the form of a picture is 'the possibility that things are related to one another in the same way as the elements of the picture'. If the picture shows a cat sleeping on a window sill then this is the form that represents a relationship between a cat and a window sill. This mention of objects and form should hopefully sound familiar (pages 18–19). What we now have, then, is the idea that a picture – made up of elements and form – represents a possible situation that might be true or false. By comparing the picture with reality we can decide whether it is true or false. This seems reasonable if we think of a picture showing a cat sitting on a sofa. We can look over at a real sofa with a cat lounging on it and confidently assert that yes, indeed, the picture is a true one. To sum up, pictures have elements (representing objects) and they have a pictorial form (representing the way objects are related to one another).

The proposition bearing the whole number 3 in the *Tractatus* says that, 'A logical picture of facts is a thought.' Facts, remember, are what make up states of affairs, the combinations of objects that constitute reality. So by saying a thought is a logical picture of facts, a connection has been drawn between thought and reality. Thoughts, of course, can be expressed through language and Wittgenstein calls the expression of a thought a proposition (like the ones that make up the *Tractatus*). This is a crucial step because what is called a proposition, the expression of a thought, can be thought of as a sentence. In other words, we are now talking about language and associating it with thought and logic.

Wittgenstein uses a metaphor to explain how a sentence is related to reality. It is a 'projection' of a possible situation. Is this projection going to work in a similar way to that of a picture? Thinking about how a projection works, this seems a likely step.

The propositions in the *Tractatus* that begin with the number 4 bring together pictures and sentences and confirm that a proposition, a sentence, represents a possible situation in a way that is similar to that of a picture representing a possible situation. So, in 4.01, Wittgenstein asserts, 'A proposition is a picture of reality.' Another analogy is introduced when he talks of the way by which musicians can obtain a symphony from a score. A music score, like a projection, is an analogy for the pictorial nature of sentences. In this way, we can understand the idea that a proposition shows its sense. It shows a possible situation

and allows for its truth or falsity. A sentence can be false but it must have sense. If I say 'The cat is on the sofa', my proposition has a sense even if the cat is asleep on a mat outside the door.

THE NATURE OF LANGUAGE

Language has a grip on reality. Names are like the co-ordinates of a point on a map. A sentence makes a claim on reality by asserting 'this is how it is'. The truth or falsity of such a claim depends only on whether what the sentence refers to really is the case or not. The truth of a sentence is not dependent on other sentences. Indeed, and this is the important point, language cannot be used to decide on its own sense. This needs to be looked at in more detail because it leads to a beguiling aspect of Wittgenstein's early philosophy.

We have been told that there are two aspects to a sentence: names and form. Objects have words, names, to represent them in a sentence and, just as a picture has pictorial form showing how objects are related in a particular combination, so a sentence has a logical form that mirrors this particular combination. If a sentence has a logical form in common with reality, then the way the names in a sentence are related must mirror the way things are related to each other in the world. At this stage you may be wondering about this idea of logical form. Presumably it is expressed through the grammar and syntax of a sentence, but what exactly is it? How, you may well ask, does the form of a particular sentence mirror the relationship between particular objects in the world? Let us look into how Wittgenstein handles this.

Wittgenstein speaks of the 'logical scaffolding' of a sentence, suggesting that the logical form of a sentence is what holds the words together in a particular formation. This particular formation, moreover, somehow mirrors the way objects are related in the real world. Wittgenstein's use of analogies such as links in a chain, projection and mapping co-ordinates support this idea that there is something logically binding and highly meaningful about the way sentences work as pictures of reality. The grip that language has on reality is tight because it is able to represent not just objects in reality but also, through its form or grammar, the relationships between objects. When I say, 'the cat is on the sofa' my proposition is not only referring to a cat and a sofa but it is also saying how they are related to one another. This is more than just a matter of throwing in a verb and a preposition. Language, claims Wittgenstein, can say things about the world because it can picture reality through its names and its form, and this linguistic picturing has all the power that Frege attributed to logic and truth.

Frege, sitting in his study with the wind howling outside, exclaimed that the truth is unassailable; it cannot be weakened by someone claiming it is not true. Wittgenstein has gone further by saying that language itself has the same unassailable quality when it is used correctly. What we would like now is a clear account of how exactly the form of a sentence mirrors the form of reality.

This, unfortunately, is something language cannot do. It can show the way reality is configured but it cannot say how it shows this configuration. Language cannot explain itself. Why not? Well, the logical form of a sentence, the relationship it represents between things, cannot itself be represented in a sentence. Why not? Well, in order to explain how the form of a sentence maps a bit of reality we can only use more sentences. These secondary sentences show what they are trying to explain because of their own form but this puts us back where we started. How do we get outside of the language in order to show how it works?

Think about how such an attempt would proceed in terms of a picture. We could include the rules of projective geometry that link a picture to its subject matter by having a small picture in the corner of the canvas showing how the projection works. But then, in order to explain how this picture of the method of projection works, we would need another picture to show how this earlier picture works. And so on, into infinite regress. It is the same with language. If we try to say what the logical form of a sentence is, we can only do so by means of a sentence that also shows this logical form – and so on, to infinity. We can show the logical form but we cannot say what it is. There is no perspective from where we can see the mirroring of reality in language. We are inside language.

'What finds its reflection in language, language cannot represent' says Wittgenstein (4.121). In order to say in a sentence what logical form is, we would have to be able to position ourselves somewhere outside logic. This is impossible: 'Logic pervades the world: the limits of the world are also its limits' (5.61).

MYSTICISM

The *Tractatus* draws to a close with a discussion of **ethics**. Propositions, remember, are pictures of the world, pictures of particular combinations of objects. These combinations

KEYWORD

Ethics: the science of morality.

possess no ethical value, they are simply states of affairs that exist. In the language of philosophy, they are **contingent**. For Wittgenstein, it follows logically that there cannot be any propositions of ethics because such propositions, to have any sense, would have to mirror something existing in reality. The form of language, given that language mirrors the form of contingent reality, simply does not allow for ethical propositions.

KEYWORD

Contingent: occurring by chance.

Well, can't we accept that the world itself is contingent, that the way objects combine is profoundly accidental, but still insist on space for an ethical attitude? Surely, Wittgenstein is not so unimaginative as to think there is no more to existing than merely occupying a piece of space in some logical-physical dimension. Quite the opposite. There is something very poetic and artistic about Wittgenstein's awareness of life and he is far from denying that there is something baffling about the world. He says, 'It is not *how* things are in the world that is mystical, but *that* it exists' (6.44). Why is there anything, instead of nothing, that is the mystery. The problem is, how can we give expression to this? We have seen how language makes sense and to use language to make ethical or philosophical statements is impossible in the same way that saying anything about logical form is impossible. It is not just that language cannot give answers to ethical or philosophical considerations; it is that it cannot meaningfully ask such questions in the first place. That is why Wittgenstein says in 6.5 that '*The riddle* does not exist'; the riddle being the mystery of life, the universe and everything. By saying it does not exist, he means it cannot meaningfully be put into words. In another, non-linguistic, sense the riddle does exist: 'There are, indeed, things that cannot be put into words. They *make themselves manifest*. They are what is mystical' (6.522). The mystery of life is there, it shows itself, but we cannot meaningfully put the mystery into words.

Wittgenstein concludes the *Tractatus* with the much-quoted words, 'What we cannot speak about we must pass over in silence'. This is proposition number 7, the last statement of the book, and the fact that it bears a whole number indicates its importance. We can use language to say what can be said, but matters of ethics and traditional philosophy cannot be spoken about in this way. So where does all this leave the *Tractatus*, for has not its own text been dealing with some of these questions? Wittgenstein does not avoid the logic of his position and the last statement before proposition 7 calmly accepts that anyone who has followed his thinking reaches the point where he recognizes them as nonsensical. They are only steps and the reader must 'throw away the ladder after he has climbed up it'. We will return to this in the next chapter.

* * *SUMMARY* * *

- Wittgenstein is captivated by the idea that language can truthfully describe the world.

- According to the *Tractatus*, the world is made up of objects that combine to form states of affairs.

- Language pictures this world: there are names for objects, and sentences have a structure that mirrors the way objects relate to one another.

- Language cannot say how it mirrors reality because we cannot get outside of language to see this mirroring.

- Language cannot speak meaningfully about ethics or philosophy. The mystery of life is just there; it lies outside of language; it shows itself.

4 A Change of Mind

TEACHER, GARDENER, ARCHITECT

The Wittgenstein who returned to Vienna after World War I had been a soldier for five years. He continued to wear his uniform as if to emphasize his haunting sense that he did not belong in civilian Austrian life. Having renounced his staggeringly large fortune, he moved out of his family house and at the age of 30 enrolled at a teacher training institution in Vienna. The author of a soon-to-be-published book, the *Tractatus*, that would create ripples of adulation in a new wave of philosophers, would become an elementary school teacher and turn his back on philosophy. He felt he was leaving nothing behind. His own thinking had concluded that what was mystical and metaphysical about life could not be meaningfully expressed in language. There was nothing that could be said about the strangeness of being in the world, trying to put it into words was literally non-sense, and philosophy was a ladder to be thrown away once one had climbed up it. Well, he had climbed the ladder – the *Tractatus* was proof of that – and now it was time to get on with a useful occupation. He needed to put the past behind him, tormented as he was by memories of his friend David Pinsent who had died so young, and he left Vienna for a school in the countryside hoping for a fresh start in life.

It was not to be. Wittgenstein the school teacher was not a happy man and for many of his pupils it was an equally unhappy experience. The cultivated intellectual from the capital was regarded with suspicion by the farming community and his rigorous and singular teaching style served to draw attention to his oddness. He boiled a dead cat and stripped off the flesh in order to teach anatomy through demonstration. Male pupils were not unused to having their ears boxed by impatient teachers, but Wittgenstein was not averse to also pulling girls' hair when they failed to respond to the two hours of arithmetic that began each day. Heads began to wag in the village. He changed schools three times but he could not adjust to what was expected of him and matters reached a crisis in 1926. Wittgenstein struck a sickly 11-year-old pupil in the classroom and the boy collapsed. Confronted by an angry parent, Wittgenstein fled the school and gave up teaching. What especially galled him was the humiliation of having to defend himself at the subsequent inquiry by lying about the extent of corporal punishment in his classroom.

Wittgenstein now seriously considered becoming a monk but settled for a period of gardening in a monastery before returning to Vienna after the death of his mother. He now embarked on a new enterprise, helping to design a new house for his sister, and applied himself to the task with his customary fastidiousness. One engineer broke down in tears trying to cope with Wittgenstein's precise instructions and on another occasion the ceiling of one room had to be raised by three centimetres before the philosopher-architect was satisfied. The house still stands, as part of the Bulgarian embassy in Vienna, but the telling details that Wittgenstein designed – unpainted radiators, doors almost half as high again as an ordinary door, door handles at shoulder height, stone floors, bare bulbs, no wallpaper – have long since succumbed to current fashions.

Wittgenstein had spent nearly six years teaching and during that time he had made one return trip to England. He renewed his acquaintance with Keynes, and although he saw Russell again they had grown apart and the relationship would never be the same as it once was. Wittgenstein's return to philosophy, when it did occur, took place in Vienna when his sister engineered a meeting between him and Moritz Schlick, a professor and leading member of what became known as the Vienna Circle.

VIENNA CIRCLE

The philosophers of the Vienna Circle were anti-metaphysical, and went so far as to reject all ideas that went beyond the ordinary,

empirical world of science. Their philosophy became known as Logical Positivism. Schlick was not the only member of the Circle to have been trained as a physicist and the influence of the natural sciences informs their cardinal principle that saying something about the world depends for its sense on there being a way of verifying whether or not it is true. Without a method of verification there was nonsense – and this left a lot of nonsense cluttering up the place. Most statements of

KEYWORDS

Empirical: based on observation or experiment alone, not on theory.

Aesthetics: the philosophy of beauty; concerned with the principles and appreciation of beauty.

Tautologies: statements that are necessarily true.

ethics, metaphysics and **aesthetics** were nonsense and the proper task of philosophy was to sweep clean and tidy up the intellectual cupboards that had become cluttered with unwanted ideas and arguments.

Wittgenstein, before ever meeting members of the Vienna Circle, had an enormous influence on their thinking. The Circle met and discussed the *Tractatus* sentence by sentence, taking from it what seemed to lend support to their empiricist, anti-metaphysical programme, and the book's author became their guru. They were especially taken by Wittgenstein's claim in the *Tractatus* about a special type of statement we haven't considered up to now. This special type of statements are the propositions of logic itself, ones that use words like 'if' and 'or'. Wittgenstein claims that such statements are saying something but they lack sense because they do not picture any possible situation. For example, in the statement 'Either there is a cat on the table or there is not a cat on the table' every situation is covered: it is true if a cat is there, but also true if a cat is not there. Being true in all situations amounts to saying nothing and Wittgenstein labelled the statements of logic as **tautologies**.

The Vienna Circle embraced this view of logical statements because it provided a way of dealing with the knotty problem of logic and mathematics. For a thorough-going empiricist, there is something intractable about the idea that mathematics and logic contains truths that appear to be universally and necessarily true. Logical Positivism wanted to say that nothing was necessarily true because the truth of anything depended on the observable facts and not some general or universal proposition. If statements of logic were tautologies then the problem was solved because, although they were true, they were not factual. If the same notion was applied to mathematics, something Wittgenstein never did, Logical Positivism had two nagging problem areas wrapped up and they could proceed to demolish the wishy-washy statements of metaphysics that lead nowhere.

What the Vienna Circle did not take on board was that Wittgenstein did not regard the ethical, or religious or metaphysical point of view – what in writing he called the mystical – as unimportant. What was mystical did not picture the world in the way normal sentences do, but then this was a logical impossibility. There was no more possibility of saying something meaningful about ethics than saying something about the logical form that sentences have in common with reality. Ethics, however, just like the logical form of language, could still show itself in the world, indeed it did show itself in the world; it just couldn't be put into words with a definite sense. This was a more ambiguous position than the Vienna Circle desired, for they wanted to stand only on solid, empirical ground. Wittgenstein did finally agree to meet with some of the Circle, and the distance between him and those thinkers who saw themselves in some respects as his disciples began to emerge. At their meetings, on occasion, Wittgenstein would read poetry to himself and poetry of a distinctly metaphysical flavour. He wanted to emphasize the fact that, although some things could not be put into the kind of propositions that the *Tractatus* was concerned with, they were nonetheless worthy of our concern.

Wittgenstein was not dismissing ethics, he was distinguishing between the kind of things language is good at representing and those things that challenge language, which seem to go beyond it, and which should not be confused with things that can be talked about in a natural way. In a letter to a publisher whom he hoped would publish the *Tractatus*,

Wittgenstein told him that the book was in two parts: the manuscript of the text was the first part while the second part was everything he had not written. And, it was this second half that was the important part. He was referring to the ethical, the mystical, which possessed a distinct boundary that separated it from the world of science. It was a failure to observe the boundary that encouraged vacuous, philosophical talk. Writing in German, Wittgenstein described such vacuous talk using a verb that is best translated as *gassing* or *babbling* and it is in this way that the *Tractatus* was therapeutic. It recognized the attractiveness of the non-sense that passed for philosophy or metaphysics and imaginatively entered this field of discourse with its own non-sense. Here, though, is where the ladder image enters the equation, as the final part of the journey to self-understanding that would end in kicking away the ladder while one was on the top rung.

This was a far cry from the rigorous empiricism of the Logical Positivists. Through the Vienna Circle, nonetheless, Wittgenstein began once more to take an interest in philosophical issues. He met with them, discussed ideas, and began to start thinking once again as a philosopher.

RETURN TO CAMBRIDGE

Towards the end of 1928, with the house for his sister near completion, Wittgenstein planned a return to England. 'God has arrived. I met him on the 5.15 train', wrote Keynes after meeting Wittgenstein at Cambridge railway station early the following year. He registered as a PhD student and depended on a university grant to make financial ends meet. Once his *Tractatus* was accepted as his dissertation, he began to give weekly lectures on philosophy and he was soon awarded a five-year fellowship that provided him with a living wage.

One of the people he met soon after returning to Cambridge was an Italian economist, Piero Sraffa. He exercised an important influence on Wittgenstein who at the time was feeling his philosophical ground beginning to shift. Sraffa, who can loosely be described as a Marxist, became a close friend and, although it is not known for sure what they discussed in their regular get-togethers, there is one story about them that would sound apocryphal were it not told by Wittgenstein himself. Sraffa was listening to his friend's account of how a sentence shared its logical form with whatever bit of reality it was referring to when he presented the philosopher with a question. Sraffa brushed the bottom of his chin with the fingertips of one hand, body language familiar to the Neapolitan as an expression of strong disdain. What, he asked, was the logical form of *that*? Maybe the author of the *Tractatus* was stumped, maybe not, but the story Wittgenstein tells shows how he found his thinking being challenged. It helps prepare the ground for the way in which the philosophy of the later Wittgenstein would concern itself with the social nature of language and the way in which meaning needs to be understood as part of a 'language-game'. This comes later but, while the shift was not as dramatic as the Sraffa anecdote might suggest, change was in the air. What did not change, although it was no longer seen in the same context, was his conviction that some aspects of the world remained ineffable, beyond any kind of rational explanation. He gave an example from aesthetics, asking what it was that made a Beethoven sonata intrinsically worthwhile. He could imagine various attempts at an answer but, he said, he would reject them all not because he had a better explanation but because they were *explanations*.

A CHANGE OF MIND

In a corny but still amusing moment in the Star Trek movie *The Voyage Home*, the ultra-logical Spock travels back in time to the twentieth century and finds himself nonplussed by a question he is asked. A woman, thinking she is engaging in a normal conversation with someone who has declined an invitation, asks him if he is sure he won't change his mind. The startled Spock, who likes to take things literally, replies by asking if there is something wrong with the one he has. The Wittgenstein who returned to teach at Cambridge was considering that there might be something wrong about the mind that had produced his earlier thinking. He didn't need advanced surgery to change it in the way that alarmed Spock, but he was going to change it nevertheless.

Wittgenstein began to question the faith he had placed in the power of logic. He started to interrogate his own assumption that there was something sublime about logic and wondered if he had not insisted on its crystalline purity because he needed it as the foundation for the account of meaning and the possibility of truth developed in the *Tractatus*. He had asserted an a priori order existing between the world and language and had insisted that this order was utterly simple. Any sentence must be either true or false, any complex proposition could be broken down into elementary statements that were true or false, and there were no assumptions lurking in the background that affected the truth of a sentence. Wittgenstein now queried this and began to think that it was like looking at what we see through a particular pair of glasses: we become accustomed to the glasses and we take for granted what we see – and it never occurs to us to take them off.

When Wittgenstein took off his conceptual glasses he saw that the sense of a sentence could depend on other things that formed part of the necessary background to a linguistic situation. Another analogy he would later introduce to explain this was that between language and a game of chess. Understanding a word was like understanding a knight or a bishop in a game of chess. It is not a matter of labelling a word as the name for a simple object in the world but rather one of understanding how the word is used and what other words are used with it. Just as explaining the meaning of a knight in chess involves explaining, or assuming an explanation is understood, of the game as a whole. This would lead to a very different philosophy, one that has become associated with the book *Philosophical Investigations*.

* * *SUMMARY* * *

- Wittgenstein abandoned philosophy and became, unsuccess-fully, a school teacher.

- After a spell of gardening in a monastery and designing a house for his sister, Wittgenstein took up philosophy once more.

- He engaged with the Vienna Circle, a group of thinkers highly influenced by the *Tractatus*.

- Wittgenstein returned to Cambridge in 1929 and started rethinking his own philosophy.

5 Philosophical Investigations

THE STRAYED POET

The *Tractatus* has considerable power, due not least to its literary style, and repeated readings bring out the temper of its austere elegance. *Philosophical Investigations*, not published until two years after Wittgenstein's death, is written in a very different style. Such are the differences in both style and content between the two books that it can seem difficult to accept that they were written by the same person. Where the *Tractatus* is self-consciously profound, terse and didactic in tone, *Philosophical Investigations* is conversational, pluralist and open-ended. The conversational aspect to the book is very pronounced and as you read the book there is no mistaking the author's awareness of the reader engaging with the text. The author of *Philosophical Investigations* wants the reader to engage with and question what is being said and there are many passages where Wittgenstein anticipates what the reader might be thinking and almost invites a response.

As an example of this, let us look at a passage where Wittgenstein is interrogating a view that was at the core of the *Tractatus* itself. The point of view in question concerns the degree of definiteness that attaches itself to the meaning of propositions. In the *Tractatus*, of course, such definiteness was built into the very nature of propositions: the relationship between objects in the world was mirrored in the form of a proposition that was true in the same way that an accurate model representation of a car accident represents the actual configuration of vehicles at the time of the accident. In *Philosophical Investigations* this view of language is questioned and found wanting and the reader is invited to participate in the process of questioning. Wittgenstein does not want to merely assert his opinion, he wants to pose questions that will linger in the reader's mind.

In the passage below, this sense of the author engaging with the reader and inviting a dialogue is enhanced by adding some imaginary responses to the selected text. The words in bold were not written by Wittgenstein but they show how a reader might respond to what is being read.

The sense of a proposition – one would like to say – may, of course, leave this or that open, but the proposition must nevertheless have a definite sense. An indefinite sense – that would really not be a sense *at all. – Hmm...Maybe. But why?* This is like: An indefinite boundary is not really a boundary at all. **Well, I guess not, if you want to be strict about it.** Here one thinks perhaps: if I say 'I have locked the man up fast in the room – there is only one door left open' – then I simply haven't locked him in at all; his being locked in is a sham. **OK. I see. I'll go along with that.** One would be inclined to say here: 'You haven't done anything at all.' An enclosure with a hole in it is as good as *none. **Hang on a minute, I'm not sure. Aren't you generalizing here?** –* But is that true? **Oh, I see, you don't really believe this yourself. I think I see what you might be getting at. The hole in a door covered by a cat flap is still part of an enclosure for a large dog. So a proposition could have an indefinite sense? Is this what you're getting me to think about?**

Philosophical Investigations 99

The tightly arranged, assertive propositions of the *Tractatus* – the author himself came to describe the book's mode as dogmatic – are replaced in *Philosophical Investigations* by questions (784 have been counted), hesitations and qualifications. Each paragraph, or a small group of paragraphs, has its own number but there are no decimal sub-divisions. The numbered sections simply follow one another, up to number 692 in the first part of the book, with no chapter divisions or titles. Commentators on the *Philosophical Investigations* use these numbers, placing them inside brackets, to refer to particular passages and the same practice is observed here in this book. Wittgenstein never put his writing into a final version for publication and it was left to his literary executors to publish his various manuscripts. It is not that Wittgenstein wasn't sure of his own ideas, rather that he was engaged in a different kind of project. He described what he was doing as drawing sketches of landscapes while journeying over a large terrain of thought. The form of *Philosophical Investigations*, like the quite different form of the *Tractatus*, is inseparable from its content. The later Wittgenstein is not seeking to propound a grand thesis and the discursive, seemingly unstructured form of *Philosophical Investigations* reflects this.

Accounts of Wittgenstein's lecturing style make clear that he also taught in an unconventional manner. Talking without notes, with long pauses for reflection, he seemed to be conducting an argument with himself. Two of his listeners penned a poem about him entitled 'The Strayed Poet'. What was Wittgenstein saying, this wandering artist who somehow found himself in the philosophy department of a university?

BABY TALK

Philosophical Investigations begins by questioning how, as infants and toddlers, we learn our language. It might seem that we learn the meanings of words by listening to adults as they point out familiar objects and their names. Grown-ups tell us about things around us and we learn how to name them accordingly. Is this why words frequently get repeated in conversations with babies and toddlers? – A cat, hmm, lovely cat. Do you like the cat? Look I can stroke the cat.

Wittgenstein does not wish to deny that this kind of language learning may on occasion take place but he wants to undermine the idea that this particular manner of language learning could be extended into a general model for the acquisition of meaning. He points out that while such an explanation may seem plausible for nouns it hardly accounts for the many other ways in which words are used. We tend to assume that other kinds of words and their grammar are somehow absorbed but that giving names to things, on the other hand, needs some kind of repeated instructions. But even in the case of nouns, does not the pointing to something and the repeated stating of its name *presuppose* the child has some language already? The child has to understand the idea that objects can have names and, in the literal case of pointing, has to understand how the pointing gesture works. If we point to a teddy bear and repeat the words, does the child then know what a teddy bear is? Does a child learn the meaning of a word like love in this way? If a parent is over-protective and possessive, a child may be learning that this is the meaning of love. If a stern parent orders a child to be quiet, the child may be learning what a command is rather than the meaning of the word quiet.

LANGUAGE-GAMES

Wittgenstein wants to criticize the view he himself put forward in the *Tractatus*, that words have fixed meanings. He asks us instead to think of words as being like tools in a tool-box, in that they each perform a different function while at the same time sharing some similarities. The analogy brings out his point that in order to understand a word's meaning we should look at the way it is used. A roof does not have the same meaning for a builder as it does for a homeless person. A person's

KEYWORD

Form of life: a term used by Wittgenstein to locate the bedrock of language in culture: in rule-governed, social forms of behaviour. A language is part of a form of life and a form of life is a fundamental given that, philosophically, has to be accepted.

name seems to have an obvious meaning but the calling out aloud of the name, depending on the tone of voice and volume, can mean many different things. How does a child come to learn that a person's name, called aloud, is often a request for their attention or a wish for that person to come towards them? A child does not learn that a person's name can be used in different ways by acts of teaching on the part of adults. Rather, words acquire meaning as part of an activity or, as Wittgenstein liked to put it, as part of a **form of life**. It is in this context that he introduces the idea of a language-game.

A language-game, as used by Wittgenstein, should not be confused with the kind of situation where one person says to another, 'oh, now you're just playing with words'. A language-game refers to a social, action-based context in which human beings relate to one another, understand one another and conduct activities amongst themselves. A language-game will have its own rules for understanding aspects of its use of language and its own internal coherence, although interesting contradictions may arise when aspects of one language-game are set alongside apparently similar aspects belonging to another language-game. An example of this, provided by Wittgenstein, is the Catholic belief in the transformation of wine into Christ's blood during the Mass ritual. The standards of evidence and proof accepted by devotees in the religious language-game are not those accepted by the same devotees in another language-game, say that of a court of law.

Much of the early part of *Philosophical Investigations*, from 1–64, concerns itself with exposing the limitations of the view of language that underpinned the *Tractatus*. Then, in 65, Wittgenstein raises an objection to the view that a word's meaning is to be found in its use or in the language-game that employs the word. Surely there must be something common to the different uses of a word, just as there must be something common to different language-games. Tell us what they have in common so that we can see what the essence of language now is. Wittgenstein answers this question by saying that different uses of language do not have one thing in common. They are related, to be sure, but they are related in a number of different ways and it is only this network of relationships that allows us to see them all as aspects of language. Nothing more. This is the profound break with the *Tractatus* because now there is no secret essence to language, no metaphysical window into the nature of the world. We are in a post-*Tractatus* world and Wittgenstein goes on to explain what the landscape of this world looks like.

FAMILY RESEMBLANCES

Sections 66 to 91 of *Philosophical Investigations* ask and answer what different kinds of games have in common. It seems an appropriate place to start because it was Wittgenstein, after all, who introduced language-games as a way of explaining how language works. So if games all have something in common then, by force of the analogy, so do language-games and therefore so does language as a whole. Surprisingly, perhaps, Wittgenstein argues that games do not have anything in common. This seems to go against common sense or, at least, it seems intuitively to be wrong somehow. Surely all games have something in common, that's why we call them games – isn't it? When we think of some of the characteristics of games – being competitive, to take one example – it does not take long to think of awkward-proving exceptions. Children play make-believe games of bringing up a baby or being doctor, or whatever, and there is no competitive element. Lots of games are co-operative in nature or purely for amusement. Games are played with other people, although even here there are exceptions (like the card game 'Patience'). Wittgenstein is not denying that all games have similarities or that we think of them as games because they show some of the characteristics we associate with games. There will always be exceptions, odd instances, and drawing the line between a game and something very close to being called a game is not always clear. For example, aspects of parliamentary democracy can seem like a game, parliamentary politics for instance, but when we think of parliamentary politics we also know that the 'game' can become very serious because ultimately it is secondary to something else. Events in Parliament, serving a more fundamental struggle for power, can have consequences that go way beyond our notion of games. Establishing a clear boundary between a game and an activity resembling a game is not possible. This is in the nature of our use of the word game. The fact that a boundary might be vague does not, however, mean that there is no boundary at all.

Games do, of course, share a set of characteristics and there is a general agreement over what can legitimately count as a game. We have this general understanding of what can count as a game because games as a whole form a 'family', with individual members resembling some other members but with no common feature shared by all members. This allows for a grey area to exist in cases where the family resemblance seems not only very weak but even open to dispute. Someone can write a play called 'The War Game' and within its literary context this use of the term game can be understood as meaningful. Calling World War II a war game, on the other hand, seems like an illegitimate use of the term game. Notwithstanding these 'border areas', what makes 'games' games is generally understood and it is this general agreement to use the term in certain situations but not others that gives the concept its stability. This is what Wittgenstein means when he says in *Philosophical Investigations* that 'the strength of the thread does not reside in the fact that some one fibre runs through its whole length, but in the overlapping of many fibres'.

BEWITCHED BY LANGUAGE

Wittgenstein uses the analogy of family resemblances to characterize the way in which games can be games by virtue of them sharing certain features and not by virtue of having to possess a particular set of features. Games and family resemblances are metaphors for the way language works. Wittgenstein wants to dramatize the difference between this new way of understanding language and the way propounded in the *Tractatus*. He no longer believes that a proposition, a sentence, possesses some essence that defines its ability to make sense. This is the point being drawn out in the passage quoted on page 37. A door with a cat flap is still a boundary even though it is a boundary with a hole in it. Language does not need perfect, idealized forms in order for it to work successfully. There is a story about Wittgenstein standing outside a building in London where someone wanted to photograph him and when he asked where he should stand he was told to stand 'roughly there'. Wittgenstein was struck by the appropriateness of the remark – the realization that standing somewhere 'roughly' was perfectly adequate – and how it could serve to say something important about language. In the *Tractatus*, he was driven to find a formal unity in language, but he now sees that such purity is unnecessary. Language doesn't work like that, it has rough edges, just as family members roughly share some characteristics.

With this new view of language comes a new view of logic. In the *Tractatus*, logic is sublime and invariant and through language it says something about the nature of the world; in the *Philosophical Investigations* there are no explanations, just descriptions. Clarity now comes, not from the invariant nature of logic, but by seeing how language works in its everyday uses. Difficulties and confusion arise because of the way we imagine language to be sublime when what is needed is a proper arrangement of language uses. It is in this context that a much-quoted remark by Wittgenstein appears: 'Philosophy is a battle against the bewitchment of our intelligence by means of language.' How does language bewitch us? The confusion is not in words themselves but in the way they are used and part of the problem is that we cannot step outside of language and survey the rules that govern language use. These rules, the grammar of a language, can be misleading and especially so if we are taken in by surface features of grammar. In the first chapter we gave an example of this when contrasting 'where is my suitcase?' with 'where is my toothache?'. If we say 'I have a pain' it is tempting to think we are using the verb 'to have' in the same kind of way as when we say 'I have a car'. Despite the similarity in their surface grammar, the two statements are not alike because they do not share the same grammar. The rules governing the use of 'have' in the sense of having possession of a car are not the same for our use of the language of pain.

You may ask, why not? I know the difference between having a car and having a pain and while I don't visit a garage to find a cure for a headache I can use the same verb in these two cases because they have something important in common. I have a car in a material, physical sense and it belongs to me. Similarly, I have a pain in my body and it belongs only to me. You can't have my pain. In one sense, this is obviously true, but at the same time Wittgenstein wants to dispute this way of thinking and show how confusing it is. If we think like this we are trapped by our language, like a fly trapped in a bottle. Philosophy, he said, if it is doing its proper job, will show the fly the way out of the bottle.

The next chapter will examine in more detail what he means by this. The consequences for philosophy, as we shall see, are far-reaching. Before we look at this, though, we will pick up the course of Wittgenstein's life in Cambridge in the 1930s, how he reacted to the outbreak of World War II at the end of that decade and what he chose to do when the war ended in 1945.

✷ ✷ ✷SUMMARY✷ ✷ ✷

● In *Philosophical Investigations* the view of language propounded in the *Tractatus* is criticized and found wanting.

● The later Wittgenstein argues that language has no sublime essence. Different language-games have different rules; different grammars.

● Philosophical problems are created by confusing different uses of language.

Letting the Fly Out of the Bottle

6

LIFE ON THE MOVE

Anecdotes about the Wittgenstein who lectured at Cambridge in the 1930s, and for a short period after World War II, have become the stuff of legend. One class that met in his bare, deckchair-furnished room at Trinity became known as 'the toothache club' because Wittgenstein liked to mine the language of pain for examples in the philosophical approach he was developing. At one stage in the early 1930s he became dismayed by the size of one of his classes, well over 30. He astonished them one day by announcing that he couldn't work with such a large number. Instead, he would dictate lectures to a select group and the lecture notes could be copied for the others. These lectures notes, bound in blue paper covers, became the first part of the posthumously published *The Blue and Brown Books*. Other typescripts and manuscripts were published after his death, including *Philosophical Remarks, Remarks on the Foundations of Mathematics, Culture and Value, On Certainty* and *Zettel*.

During this time there developed a very close relationship between Wittgenstein and one of the students chosen for his inner group, a young mathematics undergraduate named Francis Skinner. They became good friends and lovers and it was with Skinner that Wittgenstein thought of settling in Russia and becoming manual workers together. Wittgenstein did visit Russia with this in mind but the country was hardly in need of unskilled labourers and the plan came to nothing. Skinner, though, was talked out of an academic career and trained instead as a mechanic while Wittgenstein, at the end of his five-year fellowship at Cambridge, took off to Norway to work on putting his thoughts into writing. From Norway he returned to Vienna and enjoyed a happy family reunion over the Christmas of 1937 but, in both the public and private sphere, uncertainty beckoned.

Privately, Wittgenstein was sure only of the fact that he did not want to return to Cambridge. He went to Dublin, where he lived in the empty flat of a friend, and worried about his family's safety as Jews in a country that became part of Nazi Germany in March 1938. Wittgenstein, who now found himself classified as a German citizen, decided on a course of action. He applied for an academic post at Cambridge so that, with the help of his steadfast friend Keynes, he could apply for a British passport. Once this was obtained, he travelled to Vienna and helped negotiate a financial deal with the authorities that saw his family classified as *Mischlinge* (of mixed Jewish blood) and thereby safe from Nazi persecution. By now, Wittgenstein had been appointed Professor of Philosophy at Cambridge, but with the outbreak of war he was determined to do something useful for the war effort and, aged 52, moved to London to work as a porter and technician at Guy's Hospital. He later moved to Newcastle to work in the hospital there and then, towards the end of the war, to Swansea and finally, with reluctance, back to Cambridge and academic life. It was here, in October 1946, that the celebrated encounter with Karl Popper took place.

Wittgenstein and the poker

The philosopher Karl Popper, guest speaker at the Cambridge Moral Science Club under the chairmanship of Wittgenstein, has left an account of their tempestuous meeting that has been challenged in a recent book. Popper's version suggests that Wittgenstein became agitated by his inability to win their philosophical argument and took up a poker from the fireplace and challenged him to give an example of a moral rule. 'Not to threaten visiting lecturers with pokers,' replied Popper, whereupon Wittgenstein stormed out of the room in a huff. David Edmonds and John Eidenow, in their book *Wittgenstein's Poker*, investigate the incident and the backgrounds of the two philosophers with the fervour of private detectives determined to get to the bottom of a case. Witnesses contradict each other, however, and although what actually happened remains elusive there is good reason for concluding that Popper was economical with the truth.

Wittgenstein did not stay for long in Cambridge and his sense of alienation from 'putrefying English civilization', as he put it, led to him resigning his professorship in 1947 and returning to Ireland. After a short spell as a lodger with a family in Wicklow, he decided to live alone in a cottage on the west coast of Ireland – the house is now a youth hostel – in a beautiful setting surrounded by sea and mountains. He lived here for four months in the summer of 1948 but the prospect of staying there alone through the winter was too much to bear and he returned to Dublin. He spent the winter living in a hotel (now rebuilt as the Ashling in Parkgate Street), working productively and visiting Bewley's Café in Grafton Street for his customary omelette and coffee. He also sought medical advice for a growing feeling that he was not in good health but this did not prevent him making a trip to the United States. On his return, he was diagnosed as having cancer of the prostate and the last two years of his life were spent visiting and staying with friends. After a sudden collapse kept him in bed, his doctor informed him that he had only a few days to live. 'Good!' he exclaimed.

THE LANGUAGE OF PAIN

We all understand the idea of the privacy of the mind, the idea that while all sorts of things can be known about me there are always my own private thoughts and feelings that can only be securely known by myself. Only I – the bearer of the first-person pronoun – have access to my private, mental world and only when I choose to express myself through language can other people follow what I am thinking or feeling.

The use of the word 'through' in the last sentence suggests the idea that language is a tool, a means for transmitting our inner, private thoughts. This notion has a strong grip on our thinking – the use of the word 'through' seeming quite natural and appropriate – and yet it is completely rejected by Wittgenstein. Let us go back to the example – about having a pain – that brought the previous chapter to a close. Common sense would seem to reinforce the idea that only I can know from my own case what the word 'pain' means for, after all, my pain cannot be your pain. I may observe another person's behaviour and surmise that they are in pain, but only I can *know* if I am in pain. I cannot have another person's pain, just as another person cannot have my pain. This seems to be so obviously true that you might be wondering why it needs stating in the first place. It is an aspect of Wittgenstein's originality that he challenges such a deep-rooted way of thinking. Wittgenstein argues that the private ownership of pain is a misguided notion. It will be explained later why he chooses to dispute this particular area of language but for the moment let's just go along with his argument and see where it leads.

To think in terms of a pain belonging to me as opposed to a pain that belongs to you is misleading in the sort of way that it would be misleading to say that two London buses cannot have the same colour because the red of bus number 73 belongs to *that* bus, whereas the red of the number 38 bus belongs to *that* bus. Ordinarily, no one would want to make such a claim and it makes a lot more sense simply to say they have the same colour. Similarly, *my* pain is just the pain I have and, if we specify its nature (a pins and needles sensation running down my left leg), it could well be that we both have sciatica. In other words, I have the same pain that you have. The use here of the word 'have' does not signify ownership; the use of the word is more akin to its use in a remark like having a job to do or having a plane to catch.

THE PRIVACY OF THOUGHT

Why does Wittgenstein want to discuss the language of pain? In his Cambridge lectures in the 1930s, the language of pain provided him with examples that he liked to introduce as part of a broader perspective that brought into play the language of feelings. Pain is a feeling, like grief or love or hope, that seems to belong more or less uniquely to the person who experiences it. The individual case of pain can broaden out to feelings and emotions in general and the perspective can be extended even wider into questions about language and experience as a whole. All of this needs unpacking before we can see where Wittgenstein is heading.

Let us stick with the example of pain and consider an implication that arises from thinking in terms of the private ownership of feelings. If only I can know if I am in pain then it would seem possible for me – by way of a kind of thought experiment – to focus on an inner sensation, one which everyone else calls, let us say, a pain, and label it with my own private name. I could have my own rule for the use of this new word, as defined by me. For me to use this word correctly, of course, I would need to apply my private definition in a consistent manner, so that the word I choose to use today for this particular sensation carries the correct meaning when I use the same word tomorrow. Here, though, there arises an issue that Wittgenstein sees as a basic defect in any such attempt to follow through the idea of a private language. Who will decide or concur on the matter of sameness over the repeated use of the same, privately defined word? It would have to be me because it only could be me, focusing and concentrating on my inner sensation and recognizing it as the same sensation. This, though, only raises the question of consistency in another form, for how will I distinguish between consistently – correctly, in other words – applying the private definition I have given this word and merely seeming to, or thinking that I am, applying my private definition consistently? Without some independent criterion, a third party so to speak, there is only my *impression* that I am following my private definition correctly. What does an impression amount to? It means, as Wittgenstein points out at the end of section 258 of *Philosophical Investigations*, that we simply cannot talk about correctness in this case. If I am the only person who can decide that the sensation I am feeling today is the same sensation that I felt yesterday, then whatever I call the same will be the same. Who can say otherwise?

Wittgenstein argues that a private language is not possible. It won't wash, logically. If I can use the word 'same' in a way that is not open to public observation then in what sense can I use the word at all? If I insist, 'but I can clearly remember the sensation I had yesterday and it is the same as the sensation I felt today, so I am using my private word correctly', in what sense can I meaningfully be using the word 'correctly'? Well, it's correct as far as I'm concerned, you might reply. As Wittgenstein says, though, this is not how we use the word 'correctly'. You might claim you are using the word 'correctly' but claiming something doesn't make it the case. An analogy that Wittgenstein uses, in order to demonstrate the redundancy inherent in the logic that must attend the notion of a private language, is that of using your right hand to give your left hand some money. Sure, you can physically transfer some coins from one hand to another but, as Wittgenstein says, 'Well, and what of it?' (268). Another analogy he proffered was that of someone consulting a second copy of a newspaper in order to confirm the truth of what was reported in the first copy. The notion of a private language is as empty as the gestures in these examples; nothing can have the meaning aspired to if there is no acceptable way of confirming the meaning.

Wittgenstein's quip, 'Well, and what of it?', might suggest itself as a suitable comment on the entire consideration of a private language. What sane person, after all, would want a private language – so what is the value of considering it in the first place? There is a point though and it relates to the earlier discussion (pages 38–40) about baby talk and language-games. Is the meaning of a word always, unproblematically, to be found in something for which it stands – is this what words 'mean'? – and, particularly, in the case of psychological or mental terms is this something an 'inner' private experience? Or, alternatively, is the meaning of a word to be found in its use, as part of a language-game, in a way that indicates what is being expressed without recourse to some idea of making mental contact with an 'inner' something to which the word refers?

Here are some examples to consider. When the British Home Secretary stated in 2000 that he was 'minded' to release General Pinochet from house arrest he was announcing a political decision by the British government; to be single-minded is to be focused on one objective; to bear something in mind is to keep it under consideration; to be out of your mind is to behave uncharacteristically, to be seriously drunk or just to behave very oddly in some manner. In all theses cases, the notion of 'mind' is being used in different ways to mean different things.

THE GRAMMAR OF EXPERIENCE

The examples just given of the use of the word 'mind' serve to show how what Wittgenstein calls the grammar of certain psychological terms operates. Philosophical confusion arises, according to Wittgenstein, when aspects of grammar are misunderstood – and by grammar here we are not talking about the kind of errors that some school teachers like to highlight in red ink but rather how words are used in our language. We are familiar with how the word 'know' is used in a statement like 'Did you know World War II ended in 1945?' but its use is not the same in a remark like 'Did you know you had a toothache?'. The grammar of knowing in its normal sense – 'and how else are we to use it?' asks Wittgenstein in *Philosophical Investigations* (246) – includes doubting, guessing, explaining and so on but these notions cannot meaningfully be applied to the language of pain. What would it mean to visit a doctor because you have a doubt about being in pain?

All right, you might be inclined to say, I can follow this argument about the language of pain but I don't see where it is leading. Pain must be a special case because this talk of the grammar of experience doesn't apply to feelings like grief, jealousy or being in love. I can doubt, guess, explain how I feel about someone else – is it love, self-indulgence, carnal desire, am I deceiving myself? – and I need to examine my most innermost feelings to arrive at some kind of answer. With other people's feelings, on the other hand, I can observe their behaviour and expressions, make intelligent guesses, use my intuition or whatever. There is some basis for me to attribute particular feelings to other people. When it comes to my own feelings, one is still tempted to think, there must be some kind of inner observation by which I become aware of the presence of my feelings.

What happens though, asks Wittgenstein, when you observe or examine your own feelings? What is the 'grammar' of observing, say, grief in yourself? If you observe a London bus, you assert the existence of something which exists when you are not in London. This is how the word 'observe' is used. Could you also say that your grief exists even if you didn't feel it? Surely not, one is inclined to say, in which case in what sense – if any – can you observe it? Do you, asks Wittgenstein, have a particular sense that *feels* grief? Feeling your feelings – what does that mean? – and is it in any sense an act of observation?

LIFTING THE SPELL

So what is Wittgenstein getting at and where are all these questions leading? He is not reducing everything to behaviour for, while there are overlaps between **behaviourism** and what Wittgenstein is saying, he is not denying or devaluing the role of mental processes. He wants to challenge certain ideas that have run through European philosophy for centuries: the idea that while a person knows how things are with him, there is a problem area when it comes to inferring how things are 'outside' him. One such area has become known amongst philosophers as the problem of **other minds**. For Wittgenstein, however, the problem arises from thinking that subjective, private experience provides the foundations of language, the idea that words have meanings because they name language-independent thoughts and feelings.

So what is the connection between a feeling or sensation and the word we use to name it? There is a passage in *Philosophical Investigations* (244) that deals directly with this:

Here is one possibility: words are connected with the primitive, the natural, expressions of the sensation and used in their place. A child has hurt himself and he cries; and then adults talk to him and teach him exclamations and, later, sentences. They teach the child new pain-behaviour.

'So are you saying that the word "pain" really means crying?' – On the contrary: the verbal expression of pain replaces crying and does not describe it.

Note the opening qualification here. Wittgenstein is not advancing a thesis about all psychological terms but he is seeking to question the idea that words stand for inner states which only the speaker truly identifies. When he states that words are possibly connected with the primitive, he is referring to pre-linguistic behaviour. Language-games, he is suggesting, are based on pre-linguistic behaviour and it is behaviour that provides a prototype for a way of thinking and not the other way around. It is not a matter of using a word that represents an inner, private sensation, but one of replacing a behaviour, like crying for example, by an expression, 'pain', that is available in public discourse. In doing so, the child progresses from a primitive, undifferentiated cry of discomfort into a public realm that allows for differentiation; a differentiation that was not there before language. We do not access our inner life, our psychic orientation, by progressively more focused acts of introspection. Rather, we grow into a public sphere of language that allows us to access a language that opens up new discriminations and refinements of outlook.

The passage from *Philosophical Investigations* quoted above suggests a view of human experience and language that is expressive rather than cognitive and Wittgenstein uses examples from the non-human world to make this point. He asks whether a dog *means* something by wagging his tail and whether this is similar to asking whether one can say that a plant means it wants water when its leaves droop?

What is Wittgenstein getting at with these examples of tail-wagging and drooping plants? Obviously, there are vital differences between humans, dogs and plants and there is a world of difference between the wagging of a dog's tail and the kind of sophisticated introspective accounts found in the psychological novels of a Proust or a Virginia Woolf. Wittgenstein is not denying this but he does seek to deny the logical space that is always thought to exist between thought and the expression of thought. If we see a sad face we do not necessarily infer that the person is experiencing an inner state called sadness. We just see and recognize a sad face. We listen to a piece of music and call it sad. I tell you I am feeling sad. These three instances all use the same word but there is not some inner state that all three instances are referring to. Language bewitches us into thinking there must be, but look at the way words are used and the spell can be lifted.

'LOVE IS NOT A FEELING'

It is time to draw some thoughts together and let us do so by looking briefly at some other examples of psychological terms considered by Wittgenstein.

He asks whether someone could have a feeling of ardent hope or love for the space of one second, regardless of the circumstances surrounding this moment. It is not impossible to imagine a special context in which this might be imaginable for hope – recognizing your lottery number as the one that appears on the television screen (then almost instantly realizing you never purchased a ticket) – but ordinarily it is not very likely. Conjuring up a situation for a one-second experience of love is a fair bit trickier but it might not be impossible. What seems downright impossible is the idea that either such feeling could exist for such a short duration *regardless of the situation*. This is the point Wittgenstein is making, 'the surroundings give it its importance' and not some 'inner' process in the mind. The chess analogy, mentioned earlier (page 34), is appropriate here in the sense that what gives meaning or importance to the movement of an individual chess piece is not some quality that belongs to the intrinsic act of moving it but rather the 'surroundings', the rules of the game and the way a particular move acquires meaning within the context of the game being played. Take away the surroundings from the feeling of hope or love and what is left is not some nugget of pure emotion. The surroundings provide the possibility of an emotion being meaningful.

The surroundings can be as precise as the rules of a game or as broad as the possession of language and cultural norms. We can think of a dog meaning something by its behaviour because of the overlap between human surroundings and dog surroundings but a plant drooping its leaves is something else because the surroundings are so very different. As Wittgenstein says, we don't ask if the crocodile means something by coming at someone with its jaws open. The differences between human and animal behaviour are obvious but there are also some similarities and these are not so easy to discern.

'Love is not a feeling. Love is put to the test.' This fascinating remark goes to the heart of what Wittgenstein is saying about psychological terms and the way language can bewitch us with a misleading picture of human experience. Love can be pictured as a feeling that possesses one – a state of the mind or a state of the heart – and a verbal declaration of love is popularly taken as an assertion of being willingly possessed by this feeling. Only in a very limited, literary, or poetic sense is this meaningful. If you want to observe love, do not look 'inside' yourself but consider your behaviour and your attitude towards someone. Love is gauged not so much by the notion of an internal emotional barometer but tested for real by what you do in particular surroundings.

Wittgenstein is not denying that love, like many other psychological terms, is a feeling. Of course it is. But it is far more than this. Its verbal expression is a manifestation of an attitude and because its criteria are public we can observe it in other people. In the final analysis, Wittgenstein wants us to look at the way people behave and not at putative goings-on inside our minds. In the beginning was the deed, he says, not the word. Thinking and feeling manifests itself in the way we behave and conduct ourselves. Language can be seen as a kind of refinement that develops out of what he calls the weave of our life, the surroundings, the form of our life that is the culture we share. When Wittgenstein said that if a lion could speak we would not be able to understand it, he meant that the lion's surroundings, its culture, are so different to ours that we would not be able to understand its language.

* * *SUMMARY* * *

● Wittgenstein criticizes the idea that the word 'pain' refers to a private something to which only the 'I' has privileged access.

● The idea of a private language to refer to our private experiences is mistaken. Language is public and the criteria for using language coherently is public.

● Understanding is not a matter of interpreting signs into thoughts.

● Psychological terms, like love, grief, hope, are not merely feelings. They have their roots in pre-linguistic behaviour. Language has meaning in the forms of our culture.

After Wittgenstein

7

MATHEMATICS, THE TRUTH AND ALL THAT

The impact of Wittgenstein on philosophy first made itself felt through his teaching and a number of his students of the 1930s went on to establish themselves as influential philosophy teachers in their own right. Following the publication of *Philosophical Investigations* and other unfinished works and lectures that appeared after 1953, the intellectual influence of Wittgenstein spread to many university departments of philosophy in Britain and North America. Although the idea of founding a philosophical school was anathema to Wittgenstein, one could draw up an impressive list of philosophers who in one way or another could usefully be described as Wittgensteinians.

Hilary Putnam, a professor of philosophy at Harvard, has been influenced by Wittgenstein in many interesting ways. One such area concerns the philosophy of mathematics, a topic that absorbed Wittgenstein who liked to introduce examples of strange people who used methods of calculation fundamentally at odds with our most basic principles of arithmetic. Putnam is drawn to Wittgenstein's observation that there are riddles and jokes where we can only make sense of the words *after* the solution has been presented to us. In the example on the following page (not one that Wittgenstein used himself), it seems impossible that two people could be sisters, born of the same mother and father at the same hour, day and year and yet not be twins. Once we are told they are triplets, the riddle takes on sense and all is clear.

Putnam uses Wittgenstein's observation about riddles like this one to suggest that something similar could help us to understand a statement like: 'In the year 2010 scientists discovered that seven electrons and five electrons sometimes make 13 electrons.' As difficult as it is to see how

Born at the same hour, on the same day, in the same year, to the same mother and father, but not twins. How so?

such a case could possibly ever arise, it is not impossible to imagine that scientists working in a particular field might find themselves using the mathematical equivalent of triplets in such a way that 5 + 7 do not always equal 12.

Peter Winch explores the concept of a form of life in the context of anthropology and sociology. A remark by Wittgenstein – 'Show me how you are searching and I will tell you what you are looking for' – is quoted approvingly by Winch to show how a belief system has to be viewed within its own terms of reference. Take, for example, two accounts of the origins of life: a modern account like Richard Dawkins's *The Selfish Gene* and the biblical account in *Genesis*. We have the products of two different forms of life – two fundamentally different notions of how to go about understanding life – and trying to put them alongside each other would be like, says Winch, asking whether a piece of a jigsaw of the *Mona Lisa* will fit a certain position in a jigsaw of Picasso's *Les Demoiselles d'Avignon*.

What has been looked at in the last paragraph raises the alarming issue of cultural and **epistemological relativism**. Does the concept of forms of life lead to wholesale relativism? If so, this has very worrying implications. For while it is possible to imagine how someone might, from a religious point of view, 'believe' in *Genesis*, one still wants to insist that this doesn't make Creationists any less bonkers. We want to keep quotation marks around the word 'believe' because we do not want to countenance the view that Darwinism and

> **KEYWORD**
>
> Epistemological relativism: The impossibility of an uninterpreted reality that exists outside of a scheme of understanding. The idea that, because knowledge can be expressed only through a language-based conceptual scheme, the truths of one culture cannot be expressed in another, different scheme.

Creationism are somehow just two equally valid, albeit incompatible, accounts of the creation of life. If someone wants to say that they believe that *Genesis* provides a truthful account of how life was created then they are, quite simply, wrong. The best that can be said in terms of understanding what might be meant by such a point of view is that they are using a word like 'truth' in a special way.

Wittgenstein's attitude towards James Frazer's account of primitive religious beliefs in *The Golden Bough* offers a nuanced account of other belief systems that is relevant here. He criticized Frazer's reading of primitive societies on the grounds that Frazer saw the societies as somehow trying to attain a scientific outlook when really they were operating in a different field altogether. Wittgenstein said the principle behind the kind of practices that Frazer observed was to be found in 'our own soul' and not in some notion of science or rationality. By using the word 'soul', which is not being used here in its theological sense, Wittgenstein wants to draw attention to the fact that in order to understand the ritual practices of a primitive society it is necessary to draw on non-scientific attitudes and inclinations that we ourselves possess. An analogy that helps bring out the kind of distinction Wittgenstein had in mind is that of kissing the photograph of someone you feel very close to. By kissing the photograph, you are expressing a need or an emotional state of mind, not asserting belief in some causal power. In a related manner, Wittgenstein warmed to Freud for the very reasons that it has now become fashionable to criticize and dismiss him. What he liked about Freud was the very fact that he was not offering a science of the mind and that his interpretations are not open to scientific verification. Far from being concerned over Freud's use of an ancient Greek myth, Wittgenstein empathized with his ability to look at a problem from a completely new perspective, one that does not depend on the kind of causal, problem-solving reasoning characteristic of scientific thinking.

Richard Rorty, the best-known contemporary philosopher whose work explores the issues raised above, traces the line of his own thought in relation to the late Wittgenstein. Rorty regards Wittgenstein as one of the major philosophical figures whose work has decisively undermined traditional epistemology and the concomitant notion that there is an objective position from where judgement can be passed on our beliefs. Rorty, who was a teacher of philosophy at Princeton during the 1960s and 1970s, achieved fame for his views with the publication of his *Philosophy and the Mirror of Nature* in 1979. Since then, in books like *Consequences of Pragmatism*, Rorty has refined and elaborated his views and he continues to consciously evoke echoes of Wittgenstein when arguing and explaining philosophical positions with which he sympathizes.

Rorty's starting point is that, because all our accounts of the world are ultimately based on language, there is no way of getting behind or above our descriptions of the world. Our linguistic tools, our words, cannot be put alongside non-words in order to make a judgement about adequacy or correctness. A very obvious objection that one would like to make against a claim like this is to point to the achievements of modern science in understanding and predicting the nature of the physical, non-linguistic world. The post-Wittgensteinian, however, can point to the fact that physicists are no different to the rest of us when it comes to explaining objects, even sub-atomic ones, and they too offer descriptions of objects in the world. Physicists are no more able to tell us what is 'really' there than poets; science can only offer descriptions that more usefully explain the objects that are identified by our various descriptions. 'We understand matter better after Hobbes's corpuscles are supplemented by Dalton's atoms, and then by Bohr's. We understand the Mass better after Fraser, and better still after Freud', claims Rorty, but, he goes on to state, it doesn't follow that we have penetrated to the essential truth about matter or the Mass because our descriptions are better.

Rorty wants terms like appearance and reality to be thrown out with the chintz because they are outmoded, antiquated concepts that belong to a discredited metaphysics. This does not mean that Rorty wants concepts like appearance and reality to be removed from dictionaries, for they continue to serve all sorts of useful purposes in everyday life, but they have no place in a philosopher's dictionary. In an analogous kind of way, science and its mode of thinking has very obvious advantages (space travel, new medicines and so on) when it comes to making use of the causal properties of certain objects but, from a philosophical perspective, science cannot claim to offer a better understanding of these objects. There is no logical or natural stopping point when it comes to trying to understand our world and in future centuries new descriptions may emerge that offer better, more helpful, contexts for integrating our existing descriptions. Rorty characterizes those who resist this way of seeing the world as being control freaks who want to design a filing system that will have a pigeon-hole for anything that might turn up in the future.

The disappointing limitations of the kind of post-Wittgensteinian approach that Rorty endorses become apparent when considering where it may lead to and what may be made of it. Rorty himself seems content with envisaging a new kind of university where the traditional academic disciplines are replaced by a post-metaphysical, non-hierarchical order which facilitates 'conversations' between departments. Out of such exchanges of dialogues would periodically emerge new descriptions and thus new pigeon-holes for the fresh contexts. Rorty's philosophical utopia resembles a never-ending soap opera like *Coronation Street*, a varsity opera, in which the familiar story-lines and characters are constantly in the process of overlapping with novel ones, perpetually churning out new vocabularies but never reaching – because never seeking to reach – any possible core of truth.

We are already some way from Wittgenstein and the distance increases when looking at how the apparently avant-garde epistemology sketched above can be used to service highly conservative political positions. The work of the American literary critic Stanley Fish builds from the premise that everything can be reduced to contingent belief systems. Everything is 'true' only under existing conditions, truth is seen as rhetorical, and there is no position that exists outside of a particular cultural belief system. In his book *The Trouble With Principle*, published in 1999, this translates into rubbishing ideas that evoke notions like egalitarian justice and castigating wholesale the value of political principles and convictions. Fish thinks that all notions of general principles can be written off as vestiges of an old-fashioned metaphysics without realizing that his one-dimensional and politically-myopic critique amounts to another version of exactly what he himself wishes to dismiss. This manner of thinking, rejecting one kind of universalism only to replace it with another, flipside, form of universalism was something of which Wittgenstein, as we shall see in the last section of this book, was very aware.

WITTGENSTEIN AND DERRIDA

The degree of overlap between the later Wittgenstein and the French philosopher Jacques Derrida (born 1930) is a keen area of discussion in contemporary philosophy. To appreciate the philosophical nature of the relationship between these two seminal figures in twentieth-century thought, it helps to go back three centuries to *the* seminal figure in modern philosophy, Descartes.

In the seventeenth century, Descartes set philosophy on its modern course by systematically doubting everything until he thought he had reached bedrock with the incontrovertible assertion *cogito, ergo sum* ('I think therefore I am'). This was to be the starting point: the certainty of his own mind provided the foundation stone for what can be known. This philosophical perspective is known after Descartes' Latin name as Cartesian, and for some three hundred years it provided a foundation stone for Western philosophical thought.

Descartes postulated a fundamental dichotomy between the mind and the body. The mind is the anchorage point to which the first person pronoun 'I' refers: because I think, it follows that I exist. I know my own mind because this is what consciousness means. The body, on the other hand, is a separate substance altogether and one with which the mind, or the soul, interacts. Descartes located the point of interaction within a specific area of the brain. This idea, that people are made up of two quite distinct substances albeit co-existing and interacting, is known as Cartesian dualism. The history of philosophy after Descartes is in many respects a series of refinements upon this basic theme. Even though various aspects of Cartesian philosophy have been abandoned, like the religious notion of the mind as an immaterial substance, the underlying dualism is still prevalent in modern thought. The modern notion of the mind as an advanced brain state, interacting with the body through neural lines of communication, has more in common with traditional Cartesian thought than many contemporary thinkers might care to acknowledge.

The basic similarity between Wittgenstein and Derrida comes from their very radical break with traditional Cartesian thought. They share an intention to undermine metaphysical philosophy – Cartesian dualism – because of its mistaken notion that the meaning of a linguistic sign is ultimately to be located in the mind. What Wittgenstein and Derrida have in common is a rejection of the Cartesian notion that the mind has a meaning-giving ability and that this ability is rooted in self-presence. The Cartesian perspective, by locating meaning in a mental notion of self-presence, takes language out of the equation. But to be able to say *cogito, ergo sum* is to be part of a community that uses the verb 'to be', for example, in a particular, rule-governed way. It is to be part of a language community that uses grammar in a certain way. The *cogito*, in other words, presupposes a public world that exists. It would not be possible to utter the words 'I think therefore I am' unless one was already a member of a language community that possessed these words and ideas. The *cogito* cannot be a starting point for an epistemology, a theory of what can be known. Wittgenstein was once pressed by an Oxford philosopher to say whether he thought the cogito was a valid argument and he replied, 'If a man says to me, looking at the sky, 'I think it will rain, therefore I exist,' I do not understand him.'

The Cartesian picture of consciousness contains within it the notion that the mind can have access to its own contents, and experience the inner, self-present meaning that accompanies the use of language. Wittgenstein overturned this way of thinking and created the space for deconstruction.

WITTGENSTEIN AND DECONSTRUCTION

Derrida comes into philosophy from a different direction to Wittgenstein but they occupy some common ground nonetheless. Derrida, influenced by the work of Heidegger, a German philosopher whose *Being and Time* was published in 1927, aims to subvert what he takes to be a major characteristic of Western philosophy. The object of Derrida's attack is the priority given to a metaphysical notion of 'presence' – the idea that meaning arises from a kind of internal communion with oneself. When you hear your*self* speak there is felt to be a kind of certainty that breathes life and meaning into the signs of language. This, according to Derrida, accounts for a traditional and persistent notion that speech is the direct expression of thought, whereas writing is a later, second-order development in which the speaker's intentions lack the metaphysical immediacy of speech. So deeply founded is this notion that, for Derrida, it amounts to a metaphysical urge running through Western thought and one that can be discerned and traced in written works.

Working against this metaphysical urge is an inherent instability at the heart of language and Derrida's work focuses on aspects of language that bring this instability to the fore. As a consequence, Derrida looks at aspects of language that traditional philosophy overlooks – indeterminacy, metaphor, pun – in order to foreground what he calls 'the drift of signs'. Wittgenstein, incidentally, said he wanted to write a philosophical book that consisted entirely of jokes.

The above, highly abbreviated account of deconstruction elides the subtleties and sensitivities that Derrida's own writing exhibit. There are a number of qualifications that need to be added to the bald summary above, not least of which is Derrida's insistence that deconstruction is not a method or a technique. There is also the fact that deconstruction was taken up by a number of literary critics, most influentially in the United States, with the result that a deconstructionist school emerged

> **KEYWORD**
>
> Post-structuralism: a French-inspired school of philosophy that developed in the 1970s by focusing on the language-based nature of perception and thought and showing how the subject, the 'I' of discourse, *emerges* from and is constituted within language.

claiming Derrida as their intellectual figurehead. In a way that is not dissimilar to the history of the relationship between the Vienna Circle and the more nuanced ideas of Wittgenstein, some American schools of **post-structuralism** and deconstruction find in Derrida what they want to find and disregard other more intractable ideas. It helps to bear this in mind when considering the undeniable overlaps between Derrida and Wittgenstein. There are engaging similarities between the two, but it does not follow that their philosophies are identical and it certainly does not follow, as we shall see in the last chapter, that Wittgenstein was a deconstructionist.

Many interpretations of Derrida commonly attribute to him a very radical questioning, one that undermines the very idea of a decidable meaning in a text. Truth itself seems to be inherently un-decidable and this position has been elevated into a piece of post-structuralist gospel in a way that does quite some disservice to the subtlety and difficulty of Derrida's own writing. Derrida himself does not deny the importance of the way in which meaning stabilizes around and adheres to certain language uses. At the same time, he urges, this does not mean that stability can be equated with ground of incontrovertible solidity. He is saying, in other words, that sometimes language is used in a non-problematic and clear-cut way (think of a food recipe) and to always analyse it for signs of indeterminacy and instability is just plain silly. At the same time, though, it does not follow that some instances of language – those where meaning has stabilized in a unproblematic way – possess some kind of transcendental, eternal truth.

Derrida explains his practice as one of reinscribing the value of truth within 'more powerful, larger, more stratified contexts'. In language that evokes Wittgenstein's concept of forms of life, Derrida argues that the stratified contexts that constitute truths must take account of historical and materialist contexts of thought and practices. This is a long way from trendy versions of literary post-structuralism that proclaim the un-decidable nature of meaning and truth. It is not, however, unrelated to questions about the nature of certainty that Wittgenstein was thinking and writing about up to the day before he died. The idea of layers of contexts can invite speculation about the possibility of a foundation level, a fundamental layer, that would provide a bedrock of meaning and certainty. While Derrida is ready to acknowledge the importance of the way in which stability needs to attach itself to particular uses of language he is not going to invest these stable meanings with a metaphysical weight. Wittgenstein came to similar conclusions in the text that has been published as *On Certainty* where he says that the foundations that have to be exempt from doubt in any enquiry are like the hinges on which those enquiries turn. Such foundations are not mystical or metaphysical truths; it is just that we need to have some kind of foundations before we can build anything just as a door needs hinges before it can open.

Wittgenstein in art

Wittgenstein's influence is not confined to the field of philosophy. Novels, plays, poetry, biographies, film, music and art work have all been inspired by the man and his philosophy and in this respect Wittgenstein is quite unique. In Phillip Kerr's dystopian, highbrow detective thriller, *A Philosophical Investigation*, a policewoman is faced with the task of tracking down a pathological serial killer whose mind has been warped into thinking he is the early Wittgenstein. In Terry Eagleton's comic novel, *Saints and Scholars*, Wittgenstein, Nikolai Bakhtin, James Connolly and Leopold Bloom find themselves together in a cottage on the west coast of Ireland. Iris Murdoch, who went to Cambridge in 1947 in the expectation that as a philosophy research student she would encounter Wittgenstein, reveals the influence of the philosopher into a number of her novels – *Under the Net, Nuns and Soldiers* and *The Philosopher's Pupil* – although she did not find his power to be of the benign kind. Work of the Austrian novelist and playwright, Thomas Bernhard, stems from a preoccupation with his compatriot philosopher. Tom Stoppard's farce, *Dogg's Hamlet*, presents the audience with the task of grappling with an unfamiliar language-game. Derek Jarman's film, *Wittgenstein*, partly based on a screenplay by Terry Eagleton, boldly evokes the sense of alienation and wonder that seems to have haunted the philosopher's life.

✳ ✳ ✳ SUMMARY ✳ ✳ ✳

• Wittgenstein has been interpreted by contemporary American philosophers in ways that often go beyond what Wittgenstein himself intended.

• Derrida's attack on the notion of 'presence' is akin to Wittgenstein's criticism of the idea that the meaning of a word refers to an inner mental act.

• The influence of Wittgenstein has made itself felt in novels, plays and other art forms.

Idols and Not-idols

8

DOING PHILOSOPHY

Wittgenstein wanted philosophy to make a difference to how one lived one's life, and an example from his own life illustrates this point. On an occasion just before the outbreak of World War II Wittgenstein was in the company of a friend who was also a philosopher. They saw a newspaper announcement about an accusation by Germany that an assassination attempt on Hitler's life had been instigated by the British. Wittgenstein thought the accusation could have some truth to it, but his friend found it impossible to believe on the grounds that the British wouldn't act in that kind of way because it went against their national character. Wittgenstein was furious and years later wrote to his friend to explain how the incident had rankled with him. What, he explained, is the use of studying philosophy if it fails to prevent someone from thinking in such a daft way? Philosophy, he said, should improve the way one thinks and help make one careful about the use of language. He despaired to think that a degree in philosophy could enable someone to tackle questions of logic and abstruse arguments and yet prevent the same person from thinking that the British national character forbade an agency of their government planning an assassination of Hitler.

This view of philosophy as a practice that informs how we live is an enduring legacy of Wittgenstein. He did not invent the idea that philosophy should shape how we conduct our lives; we have only to think of Socrates resisting his friends' suggestion to flee Athens, after being condemned as an enemy of the state, and choosing instead to take his own life. The French philosopher Pierre Hadot has written an enticing book, *Philosophy as a Way of Life*, about the long and partly buried tradition in Western thought that sees philosophy as a mode of existing-in-the-world. Hadot explores the role of spiritual exercises – philosophical meditation as something practised and lived – in ancient Greek and Roman philosophers. He relates this tradition of philosophy as a therapeutic practice to some modern thinkers. Interestingly, in his final lecture at the Collège de France in 1991, Hadot told his class that after three decades of teaching he had come to the conclusion that we can scarcely talk about what is most important. Consciously echoing Wittgenstein, he said how he felt that putting into words the mystery of life was doomed to inadequacy because language simply cannot directly communicate some impressions and experiences. Poets and other artists can open doors of perception into existential questions about life and death, but only fleetingly. The unsayable remains unsayable, not in a literal sense but in a meaningful sense. Some aspects of life – the more profound aspects – lie outside language.

The concern with language is common to the early and late Wittgenstein. It provides for him the bedrock that gives philosophy its identity and its purpose. The limits of language are the limits of our world in both the *Tractatus* and *Philosophical Investigations*. For Wittgenstein, there are no problems in philosophy, only puzzles that can be traced back to the nature of language. One of his analogies for understanding language takes us into the driver's cabin of a steam locomotive and its manifold handles and their apparent uniformity:

> But one is the handle of a crank which can be moved continuously (it regulates the opening of a valve); another one is the handle of a switch, which has only two effective positions, it is either off or on; a third is the handle of a brake-lever; the harder one pulls on it, the harder it brakes; a fourth, the handle of the pump: it has an effect only so long as it is moved to and fro.

It is possible to think a handle is doing one thing when actually that is not its function and puzzles arise in philosophy when practitioners treat a word or a concept in a way it is not supposed to operate. Puzzles are created, said Wittgenstein when 'language goes on holiday' and he thought plenty of examples could be found in the dry articles of learned philosophy journals. He never made a habit of reading them, much preferring the laconic style of American pulp fiction, and he told a friend that bad philosophers were like slum landlords and his job was to put them out of business.

HOUSES OF CARDS

Walking one day in Dublin's Phoenix Park, Wittgenstein told his companion that the philosopher Hegel wanted to show how things that look different are really the same whereas he wanted to show the opposite. A quotation from *King Lear* – ' I'll teach you differences' – came to his mind as a possible epigraph for *Philosophical Investigations*.

Wittgenstein's concern with language and its differences, with what can and cannot usefully be said, links the thought of the *Tractatus* with that of his later work. A concern with language is also what characterizes deconstructionist thought but the uniqueness of Wittgenstein's thought is encapsulated in the following remark of his:

> All that philosophy can do is to destroy idols. And that means not creating a new one – for instance as in 'absence of an idol'.

For Wittgenstein, philosophy was a form of therapy – he compared it in one instance to Freudian psychotherapy – that exorcized the errors of thinking metaphysically by turning what was latent nonsense into patent nonsense. This is his point in exploring the language of pain, the notion of a private language and so on – to bring out, as he puts it, the bumps 'that the understanding has got by running its head up against the limits of language'. It is not part of the therapy to replace one kind of illusion – that meaning resides in some kind of mental essence – by another illusion that is simply based upon a denial of the first illusion. Creating some profound identity out of terms like the 'undecidability of meaning' or the 'impossibility of truth' is a mirror inversion of the first illusion that meaning and truth reside securely inside the mind.

Destroying all notions of meaning or truth is as metaphysical as imbuing them with transcendental meaning in the first place. This is what Wittgenstein means in the above quotation about destroying idols and replacing them with a new one based on the absence of an idol. He does not seek to replace one (false) belief with another (equally false) belief based on its negation. This is the gap between deconstruction and Wittgenstein. To elevate to the status of a truth the claim that there is no truth is not the kind of paradox that Wittgenstein wants to embrace. To assert that there is just an endless and unstoppable play of language forms, investing the core of our forms of communication with an irremediable undecidability, is not a Zen-like paradox. It is a kindred form of metaphysical confusion.

Wittgenstein does conceive of philosophy as a destructive activity, but destruction as a form of therapy. He expresses this vividly in *Philosophical Investigations* (118):

> **KEYWORD**
>
> **Plato's cave:** Plato, in the *Republic*, introduces the analogy of prisoners in a cave to represent the state of the philosophically unenlightened. The prisoners can only see moving shadows and they mistake these shadows for the whole of reality itself. The world outside the cave represents the Forms, the underlying essences – the universals – that account for the particular things that we describe when referring to these Forms. So, for example, behind the various cases of a just individual, a just social system, a just tax and so on, there must be something called Justice.

> Where does our investigation get its importance from, since it seems only you destroy everything interesting, that is, all that is great and important? (As it were all the buildings, leaving behind only bits of stone and rubble.) What we are destroying is nothing but houses of cards, and we are clearing up the ground of language on which they stand.

The therapeutic value of philosophy arises from the realization that what is being destroyed has no substance to begin with; the supposed substance is mere houses of cards. A metaphysical concept like Cartesian dualism is an example of such a house of cards and Wittgenstein is at one with deconstruction in this respect.

Philosophy, for Wittgenstein, will lead one out of the cave of illusions, but not into a world of Forms, for **Plato's cave** is not a starting point. Instead, philosophy will lead one into a world of forms of life, language-games and family resemblances. A world without idols but also a world without a new set of philosophical illusions built on the negative foundations of not-idols. In this respect, Wittgenstein parts company with deconstruction. Houses of cards arise from the wish, the need, for what is 'great and important', but what is important is recognizing the meaningful sense in which philosophy is not about greatness.

GLOSSARY

A priori (literally, 'from what is prior') what is known independently of experience, as opposed to knowledge which can only be justified by some appeal to experience. For example, the claim to know that 'the dog is by the door' is justified by observation of the dog in question.

Aesthetics the philosophy of beauty; concerned with the principles and appreciation of beauty.

Behaviourism the theory that accounts of mental states can be given in terms of behaviour rather than thoughts or feelings. The theory is often used in arguments against dualism by accounting for the mental in terms of physical, publicly observable behaviour.

Contingent occurring by chance, neither necessary nor impossible. Whether a statement is contingently true or false is one where the truth or falsity depends on circumstances; it may be true or it may be false. A statement which is necessarily true, on the other hand, is true under all circumstances.

Descartes French philosopher (1596–1650) who aimed to establish a clear basis for certainty by pushing doubt to its extreme, until he reached a point where doubt was no longer possible. This point, he reasoned, was expressed in his principle *cogito, ergo sum* ('I think therefore I am') and from it he built up his body/mind dualism.

Dualism the theory that reality consists of two basic and distinct substances or entities: one mental and one physical. Such a theory gives rise to various accounts of the nature of the relationship between the two substances.

Empirical based on observation or experiment alone, not on theory. Summed up in the maxim: nothing is in the mind which was not first in the senses. In the history of schools of philosophy, empiricist accounts are opposed to those that rest on the idea that some of our knowledge of the world takes the form of innate ideas.

Epistemological relativism the impossibility of an uninterpreted reality that exists outside of a scheme of understanding. The idea that, because knowledge can only be expressed through a language-based conceptual scheme, the truths of one culture cannot be expressed in another, different scheme.

Epistemology the theory of knowledge and what, if anything, counts as knowledge. Epistemology considers what conditions have to be fulfilled in order for a claim of knowledge to be justified, as opposed to mere belief. This raises, in turn, the question of what counts as justification and there is no agreement on this. The philosophy of the later Wittgenstein questions whether a justification is always called for.

Ethics the science of morality.

Form of life a term used by Wittgenstein to locate the bedrock of language in culture: in rule-governed, social forms of behaviour. A language is part of a form of life and a form of life is a fundamental given that,

philosophically, has to be accepted.

Frege German philosopher (1848–1925) who worked on the foundations of mathematics in the hope of deriving the basic principles from pure logic. Wittgenstein's conversations with Frege led to the young Austrian seeking out Bertrand Russell at Cambridge.

Freudian arising from the work of Sigmund Freud, who worked in Vienna at the end of the nineteenth and beginning of the twentieth century; especially associated with the importance of sexuality in understanding human behaviour.

Keynes John Maynard Keynes (1883–1946), English economist, proponent of state-managed full employment under a capitalist system.

Language-game a term introduced by Wittgenstein to highlight the way in which language use is a form of social, rule-governed activity bounded by a context and a set of human purposes.

Metaphysics the study of the ultimate nature of reality, of what cannot be examined through experiment and observation. When the works of Aristotle were being organized his students labelled the book following the one on physics, or nature, 'metaphysics' (literally, the one coming after). Metaphysical enquiry concerned solely with the nature of being is called ontology (from the Greek for 'beings').

Mysticism a meaning that is hidden, mysterious, spiritually apprehensible.

Other minds a problem in the theory of knowledge about how – or even, if – one can know or justifiably believe that other people have thoughts and feelings.

Plato's cave Plato, in the *Republic*, introduces the analogy of prisoners in a cave to represent the state of the philosophically unenlightened. The prisoners can only see moving shadows and they mistake these shadows for the whole of reality itself. The world outside the cave represents the Forms, the underlying essences –

the universals – that account for the particular things that we describe when referring to these Forms. So, for example, behind the various cases of a just individual, a just social system, a just tax and so on, there must be something called Justice.

Postmodern a self-awareness in art of the forms of art themselves; the tendency in literature, architecture and other arts to adopt an ironic attitude towards its own identity.

Post-structuralism a French-inspired school of philosophy that developed in the 1970s by focusing on the language-based nature of perception and thought and showing how the subject, the 'I' of discourse, emerges from and is constituted within language.

Private language the private language argument arises from the question of whether it is possible for a language to consist of elements which it is impossible for anyone but its speaker to understand. The argument's importance is often raised in relation to sensations, like pains for example, which have been thought to refer to private experiences. Wittgenstein argues that to use a language involves some notion of correctness and incorrectness and this depends on the possibility of being able to check that one is using words correctly. The use of a private language does not allow for such checking and is therefore seen to be impossible.

Proposition in philosophy, a proposition is not a 'proposal' in the ordinary sense of the word. It usually refers to the thought being expressed when a statement or claim is made that something is the case. So, for example, 'all pacifists are non-violent' expresses the same thought, the same proposition, as 'no pacifists are violent'. Strictly speaking, a proposition is not the same as a sentence although it may often be taken to refer to the same idea. The words 'angry dandelions sleep peacefully' certainly look like a sentence but they do not constitute a proposition because no sensible statement is being made.

Realism the view that draws attention to the existence, the reality, of things and objects. It is best understood in relation to views it opposes, like the view that displaces the things in question in favour of ideas or words.

Russell Bertrand Russell (1872–1970), an English philosopher, who taught at Cambridge where he met Wittgenstein as one of his students before the First World War. Russell recognized his talent, remarking: 'His avalanches make mine seem mere snowballs'. In later years, however, they grew apart both personally and philosophically.

Sense data entities which exist only because they are sensed by us. Examples of sense data commonly provided include smells, taste, colour patches. The plural of sense datum (literally, 'given to sense').

Tautology a tautology (literally, 'saying the same thing') is a statement which is necessarily true due to the repetition of a word or symbol. The term may be used in a strict sense to refer to logical truths such as 'the sky is blue or the sky is not blue'.

FURTHER READING

Wittgenstein, L., *Tractatus Logico-Philosophicus* (first published 1921; London 1961), *The Blue and Brown Books* (Blackwell, 1958), *Philosophical Investigations* (first published 1953; Blackwell, 1958), *Zettel* (Blackwell, 1981), *On Certainty* (Blackwell, 1969)

Hadot, Pierre, *Philosophy as a Way of Life*, Blackwell, 1995
Not a book about Wittgenstein as such but he lurks philosophically in the background (see pages 69–70).

Eagleton, Terry, *Saints and Scholars*, Verso, 1987
A highly witty piece of fiction which brings together four noted individuals, one of whom is Wittgenstein (see page 67).

Crary, Alice and Read, Rupert, (eds), *The New Wittgenstein*, Routledge, 2000
A collection of essays by academics dealing with various aspects of the early and late Wittgenstein. Ones to read include those by Stanley Cavell and Hilary Putnam. Two others, Martin Stone's 'Wittgenstein on deconstruction' and Alice Crary's 'Wittgenstein's philosophy in relation to political thought', have been drawn upon in the final two chapters of this book.

Monk, Ray, *Wittgenstein*, Vintage, 1991
Justly praised biography of Wittgenstein that successfully manages to present the philosopher within the context of his age without losing sight of the uniqueness of the man and his ideas.

Wittgenstein, The Terry Eagleton Script/ The Derek Jarman Film, British Film Institute, 1993
The two scripts of the film: Eagleton's realist one and Jarman's experimental one. This book is well worth seeking out, not least for the intelligent introduction to Wittgenstein by Eagleton that accompanies the two scripts and, even if the film has not been seen, there is a selection of photographs that capture the style of Jarman's approach. A video of the film itself is available through the BFI.

Eagleton, Terry, 'Wittgenstein's Friends' in *Against the Grain*, Verso, 1986

An essay, first appearing in *New Left Review*, exploring the interconnections between Wittgenstein, post-structuralism and historical materialism.

Wall, Richard, *Wittgenstein in Ireland*, Reaktion Books, 2000

The most detailed account available of the philosopher's sojourns in Ireland, accompanied by photographs of the places where Wittgenstein stayed and some of the people he met while living in the country. Wittgenstein visited Ireland on five occasions, spending almost two years there altogether. His longest visit was in 1947, after he had given up his professorship in Cambridge. He played with the idea of settling in Ireland's capital, Dublin, and considered the notion of training to become a psychiatrist. He felt he could live in Dublin, although he was not drawn to the city's Georgian architecture: 'The people who built these houses had the good taste to know that they had nothing very important to say, and therefore they didn't attempt to express anything.' What Wittgenstein did take a liking to was Bewley's Cafe – which is still there in Grafton St in the heart of the city – not least because the waitress came to recognize him and would deliver his omelette and coffee to his table without being asked.

Edmonds, David and Eidinow, John, *Wittgenstein's Poker*, Faber and Faber, 2001

A good book to read if coming to Wittgenstein with little previous knowledge of the historical, social and intellectual contexts in which he lived. Subtitled 'The story of a ten-minute argument between two great philosophers' (see page 46 for a brief account of the contentious encounter between Wittgenstein, Popper and a poker), this is a lively and very readable study. What makes it particularly engaging is its ability to use the poker incident as a springboard for exploring the life and times of the two men and what lay behind their loud and aggressive confrontation in a crowded room in Cambridge in October 1946.

Cornish, Kimberley, *The Jew of Linz*, Century Books 1998

See page 12 for an account of this book's argument that makes the young Wittgenstein the actual Jew that Hitler refers to in *Mein Kampf*. The evidence is circumstantial and convincing to a degree; more suspect are the claims that the author goes on to make about Wittgenstein.

DESCARTES –
A BEGINNER'S GUIDE

Kevin O'Donnell

Descartes – A Beginner's Guide introduces you to the so-called father of modern philosophy. This introdution seeks to establish why that should be so. He lived at a time of new scientific ideas and discoveries and he provided the philosophical framework that guided the newly emerging study of science.

Kevin O'Donnell's lively text explores:

- the social and intellectual concerns of Descartes' life and work

- major events in the life of the philosopher

- Descartes' key ideas about the dualism of mind and body

- Descartes' scientific contributions, and the establishment of scientific method.

The facts ... the concepts ... the ideas ...

MARCEL PROUST – A BEGINNER'S GUIDE

Ingrid Wassenaar

Marcel Proust – A Beginner's Guide introduces you to the life and works of Proust. He is shown as a writer who has influenced not only the way we approach literature but also the way we think about ourselves. Discover how *A La Recherche du Temps Perdu* is relevant to today's technology-intensive and individualistic society.

Ingrid Wassenaar's lively text explores:

- how to approach *A La Recherche du Temps Perdu* (In Search of Lost Time)

- Proust's ideas on topics such as time, memory and sexuality

- modern critical approaches to Proust and his ideas

- the relevance of these ideas to readers in the twenty-first century.

The facts … the concepts … the ideas …

DOSTOYEVSKY – A BEGINNER'S GUIDE

Rose Miller

Dostoyevsky – A Beginner's Guide introduces you to the life and works of Dostoyevsky. Explore the range and versatility of this thought-provoking and compelling writer, focusing on his concern with writing as a means of understanding the human condition.

Rose Miller's lively text offers:

- an insight into the relationship between the writer's life and his work

- an exploration of characteristic featires and recurrent themes in his writing

- an outline of some helpful critical approaches to his style

- an analysis of *Crime and Punishment*, *The Idiot* and *The Brothers*.

The facts … the concepts … the ideas …

FREUD –
A BEGINNER'S GUIDE

Ruth Berry

Freud – A Beginner's Guide introduces you to the 'father of psychoanalysis' and his work. No need to wrestle with difficult concepts as key ideas are presented in a clear and jargon-free way.

Ruth Berry's informative text explores:

- Freud's background and the times he lived in
- the development of psychoanalysis
- the ideas surrounding Freud's work on the unconscious.

The facts … the concepts … the ideas …

JUNG – A BEGINNER'S GUIDE

Ruth Berry

Jung – A Beginner's Guide introduces you to the 'father of analytical psychology' and his work. No need to wrestle with difficult concepts as key ideas are presented in a clear and jargon-free way.

Ruth Berry's informative text explores:

- Jung's background and the times he lived in
- the development of Jungian analysis in simple terms
- dreams and their interpretation
- classic interpretations of popular myths and legends.

The facts … the concepts … the ideas …